CANADIAN MEDICAL LIVES NO. 6

EMILY STOWE
Doctor and Suffragist

MARY BEACOCK FRYER

Series Editor: T.P. Morley, M.D.

Hannah Institute
&
Dundurn Press
Toronto and Oxford
1990

Design and Production: JAQ
Copy Editor: Mark Fenton
Printing and Binding: Gagné Printing Ltd., Louiseville, Quebec, Canada

Dundurn Press wishes to acknowledge the generous assistance and ongoing support of **The Canada Council, The Book Publishing Industry Development Programme** of the **Department of Communications** and **The Ontario Arts Council.**
 Care has been taken to trace the ownership of copyright material used in the text, including the illustrations. The author and publisher welcome any information enabling them to rectify any reference or credit in subsequent editions.

J. Kirk Howard, Publisher

Canadian Cataloguing in Publication Data

Fryer, Mary Beacock, 1929–
 Emily Howard Stowe

(Canadian medical lives ; no. 6)
Includes index.
ISBN 1–55002–084–6

1. Stowe, Emily Howard, 1831–1903.   2. Women physicians – Canada – Biography.   3. Suffragettes – Canada – Biography.   4. Women – Suffrage – Canada.
I. Hannah Institute for the History of Medicine.
II. Title.   III. Series.

R464.S76F78 1991   610'.92   C90–095731–X

Dundurn Press Limited
2181 Queen Street East
Suite 301
Toronto, Canada
M4E 1E5

Dundurn Distribution
73 Lime Walk
Headington
Oxford, England
OX3 7AD

CANADIAN MEDICAL LIVES SERIES

The story of the Hannah Institute for the History of Medicine has been told by John B. Neilson and G.R. Paterson in *Associated Medical Services, Incorporated: A History* (1987). With the creation of the Institute the AMS endowed it with funds, capability and responsibility to develop and disseminate a body of medical history hitherto hidden in the country's memory.

A grants and personnel support program enables the Institute through medical, social and political historians to become a powerful influence in the rapidly expanding interest accorded to medical history. A chair in the history of medicine is supported at each of the five Ontario medical schools.

Originally the Institute's support was limited to Ontario, but it has now been extended to medical historical work in any part of Canada.

Dr. Donald R. Wilson, President of Associated Medical Services, persuaded the Board that the Hannah Institute should launch a series of biographies of those who, as yet unsung, had made major contributions in the broad field of Canadian medicine during their lifetime or who, for other reasons, were notable in their day. The Institute also had in mind for the series members of the nursing profession, particularly those who had pioneered public health services, as well as workers in related fields.

Mary Fryer's story of Emily Howard Stowe is an account of a determined and talented woman who became both the first female school principal and the first Canadaian woman to practice medicine in Canada. She was involved in the struggle for the enfranchisement of women and their access to education.

The next volumes in the Canadian Medical Lives Series include Francis A.C. Scrimger (Suzanne Kingsmill), R.G. Ferguson (Stuart Houston), J.C.B. Grant (C.L.N. Robinson), and Earle B. Scarlett (Bill Mussellwhite).

There is no shortage of meritorious subjects. Willing and capable authors are difficult to acquire. The Institute is therefore deeply grateful to the authors who have already committed their time and skill to the series.

T.P. Morley
Series Editor
1990

CANADIAN MEDICAL LIVES SERIES

*published

CANADIAN MEDICAL LIVES NO. 6

EMILY STOWE
Doctor and Suffragist

MARY BEACOCK FRYER

Series Editor: T.P. Morley, M.D.

CONTENTS

ACKNOWLEDGEMENTS

THE DEBT TO DR. STOWE'S grandson, Hudson Stowe, in preparation of this work is incalculable. Hudson is the family genealogist, as well as the owner of a vast collection of newspaper clippings and other materials. In addition, he donated scrapbooks to Wilfrid Laurier University, family papers to Victoria University, and the Peter Lossing papers to the Metropolitan Toronto Library. He read each chapter as it was written, frequently adding anecdotes and correcting errors.

Another helpful person is Joyce Pettigrew, archivist with the Norwich and District Archives. She gave unstintingly of her time to ensure that everything of value in Norwich was available. A day spent exploring the places Dr. Stowe knew, would not have been as valuable without Mrs. Pettigrew's advice.

The staff members at Victoria College were so careful of the Stowe material that they instilled the same guilt feelings as in undergraduate days. More trusting were the librarians at the Academy of Medicine, who went to great lengths to find obscure data.

INTRODUCTION

EMILY STOWE IS REMEMBERED, foremost, as one of Canada's earliest and most determined suffragists, rather than as a doctor. She steered her own course more in the direction of acquiring political power than towards any particular contribution to expanding medical knowledge. In fact, Dr. Stowe is worthy of inclusion in this series of medical biographies, not so much for what she did as a doctor, as for her accomplishment in ever becoming a medical practitioner at all.

She was a pioneer in two fields, as a woman doctor, and as a crusader for women's rights. The sources on her activities for the latter cause are much more extensive than for the former. The material specifically relating to Dr. Stowe as a practitioner is sparse, but sources on conditions of medical practice during her years as a doctor are plentiful and help to place her in her proper context. From such sources it was possible to reconstruct what life was like as a practitioner, male or female, in the second half of the nineteenth century.

Medicine at that time was hardly scientific in the modern sense. The chief feature of medical practice was the observation of the patient, and the doctor's equipment was rudimentary. The application of the scientific method to the study of diseases lay in the future. Both diagnosis and treatment were still often a matter of fortuity, sometimes with satisfactory results. While little is known of Emily Stowe as a doctor, a wealth of information exists on her concern with social issues.

In biographies of woman doctors in the United States during the mid-nineteenth century, four themes recur. These are the franchise, female education, temperance, and the abolition of slavery. For Emily Stowe, a Canadian studying in the United States following abolition, the first three were still burning issues. Later experience convinced her that the first — enfranchisement — was the key to achieving the other two. Emily Stowe the suffragist has come to overshadow Emily Stowe the doctor. Yet the latter role was as vital to Emily herself; it was the cause that launched her into the struggle for women's rights.

Dr. Stowe stands out against a backdrop of Victorian Canada. Modern readers may be tempted to call her a feminist, a term now in vogue, and to criticize her for setting circumscribed limits to her aspirations. That would be like asking her to fly before she could walk. Many of the reforms Emily advocated were intended more to improve the quality of the home than to encourage women to leave their homes for the work place. She did not envisage a time when women would seek to enter all the fields hitherto confined to men; male and female each had his or her own "sphere."

Emily Howard Jennings Stowe, M.D., 1831–1903. Painting by Lorraine B. Hovey, and donated to the Women's College Hospital by Emily's grandson, Hudson Stowe. (Courtesy Women's College Hospital)

ONE

Equal Among Friends

EMILY HOWARD JENNINGS STOWE (1831–1903) was nurtured and sustained by a family background and upbringing which taught her that woman was the equal, in every respect, of man. A resounding beginning to her biography would be to proclaim her as Canada's first woman doctor. However, someone would likely raise the question of Dr. James Miranda Stuart Barry.

No one knows the real name of Dr. James Barry (1790?–1865). Disguising her sex, she entered the medical school at Edinburgh, Scotland, in 1809, graduating in 1812. Later she joined the British army as a medical officer. In 1857, Dr. Barry arrived in Canada as Inspector-General of [military] Hospitals after a career that had taken her to many places where British interests were involved. Only after her death in London in 1865, as her body was being prepared for burial, was her secret revealed. At the time, men declared that since a woman was not capable of being a doctor, she was a male hermaphrodite.[1] Because of him/her, Doctor Stowe should be remembered as the first Canadian woman to practise medicine in Canada. Dr. Barry disguised herself out of a strong conviction that a woman had much to contribute to the field of medicine. Dr. Stowe shared this conviction as she went in quest of the qualification — as a woman.

Emily Stowe came of Quaker stock. Added to the Quaker outlook was Dutch tolerance. Eight generations back, in 1658, her ancestor,

Pieter Pieteresse Lassingh, had left Holstein for the colony of New Netherland (now New York State). Lassingh's native land was known as the most liberal country in Europe; Jews, Huguenots, and English Puritans all found sanctuary and religious freedom in Holland. Soon after Pieter arrived in the New World, Lassingh became Lossing, a surname of modest historical interest in Canada and the United States.[2]

By the sixth generation there were two Benson Lossings, one in Upper Canada and the other in New York State. The first was her great-uncle Benson (1799-1881) a brother of Emily's grandmother, Paulina Lossing Howard. The second was Paulina's first cousin, Benson Lossing (1813-1891), the American wood engraver, author and editor best remembered for his copiously illustrated field books of the American Revolution, the War of 1812 and the United States Civil War. The best known Canadian Lossing is Solomon (1784-1844) an elder brother of Paulina and the first Benson Lossing. At the time of Emily's birth, her great-uncle Solomon was convinced of the urgent need of political reform in Upper Canada.[3]

Dr. Stowe's branch of the Lossing family were Quakers who came, with other members of the Society of Friends, from Dutchess County, New York, to Upper Canada in 1810, because they had bought good land. They were led by Peter Lossing, of the fifth generation from Pieter Lassingh, and his brother-in-law Peter DeLong (Lossing's second wife was Catherine DeLong). The year before, in 1809, Peter Lossing had come, with Peter Stover, to York (now Toronto), where they arranged to purchase 15,000 acres in the new Norwich Township, from a man named Wilcocks. This was a Crown grant to Wilcocks. When Peter Lossing returned to settle, he brought some of his children, but not Emily Stowe's grandmother, Paulina. She had married Henry Howard, of Cranston, Rhode Island. Henry was ill when the others set out, and the Howards were unable to travel with them. He died before the end of the year, leaving Paulina with a year-old daughter, Hannah.

Paulina moved to her in-laws home in Cranston, while her father and brothers were clearing land and building their first house in the bush. Peter Lossing wrote to his "far distant daughter" on the twenty-fourth of October expressing his sympathy over the death of Henry Howard, asking her to give his love to "precious little Hannah. Kiss her for me. Tears ... blur the paper so I cannot write much more." By March, 1811, Peter had a two-storey house on his land and Paulina's mother and sisters moved there. They had stayed with friends beforehand in nearby Burford Township. By November 1811, Peter was so well settled that he was expecting Paulina to join her family the next season. The Quaker community now amounted to seventeen families. Within a two and a half mile radius of Peter's farm lived 150 "souls." The markets were good. Wheat fetched $1.25 a bushel, corn 75 cents, pork $7.00 to $7.50 a hundredweight, beef $4.50 to $5.00, butter 15 cents, cheese 12 cents. Cloth was cheap; calico could be bought for from 18 to 50 cents a yard.[4]

By the next season, the United States had declared war on Britain, and Paulina was cut off from her family for the duration, except for one brother, John, who had remained in New York State to serve out an apprenticeship. By the twenty-fifth of February, 1815, before Peter Lossing knew that a peace treaty had been signed, he was searching for a way to bring Paulina and Hannah to Norwich:

> We have been much favoured thus far as it respects the din of War, although on every side of us within 2 or 3 days travel several battles have taken place yet our little settlement has suffered scarcely anything in person or in property. I have still a good Lot of 200 acres of land reserved for thee within a few miles of me, and a very welcome home for thee and little Hannah ...

He explained that some Quakers had received permission of the government to go to New York for the Yearly Meeting. One Samuel Taylor, going to Philadelphia, would post the letter:

> I doubt not but a permission might be obtained for thee and the child to pass the lines with them [the Quaker delegates] either to the bay of Quinte to the Dorland neighbourhood or to Black Rock, Buffalo — into the compass of our Monthly Meeting — if any difficulty should arise as those Friends will come on horseback — in the expense of joining them with another Horse and Waggon — for want of means any assist-

ance those friends should see proper to afford thee I will re-
pay to them on their return, and if it should not be permitted
for you to cross with Waggon and horses they might be sold
or left at Willink [near Buffalo] — among a settlement of
Friends. From thence you might readily cross with a Flag...

He advised Paulina to bring very few possessions as that might be
unsafe. On the exterior he had written, "The Postmaster will have the
goodness to forward this from a Father to a beloved daughter far
separated."[5] He probably meant the postmaster in Buffalo, and that he
had found the means to smuggle his letter across the border since
regular mail between the two countries was intercepted. By March,
knowing the war was over, Peter arranged for Paulina's brother John
to escort her to Upper Canada. On the eighteenth he wrote, " ...All our
settlers [are] well satisfied both with the Government we live under
and the country the mildness of the British Constitution." Although
invading armies had marched all around the settlement, the young
Quaker men were neither compelled to enlist, nor fined. Some, however, volunteered to build a fort (really a blockhouse) at Long Point
and to guard grist mills near their homes.[6]

Paulina made the journey with the now six-year-old Hannah. At
first she stayed with her parents, but she soon met a fellow Quaker,
George Southwick. Paulina and George were married at the Monthly
Meeting at the Friends' meeting house in Pelham Township on the
thirteenth of December, 1815. Both were listed as residents of Norwich
where there was as yet no meeting house. By 1820, George owned Lots
4 and 5, Concession 12 — 400 acres in all — in the southeast corner of
Norwich Township, Oxford County, in the London (administrative)
District.[7] His stepdaughter, Hannah Howard, returned to the United
States when she was sixteen to attend the Friends' Yearly Meeting
Boarding School in Rhode Island, more often called the Providence
Seminary.[8] Like all Quaker schools it was a coeducational establish-
ment. There she received the excellent education she was able to pass
on to her children, who grew up in a pioneer community that had no
adequate schools.[9] Hannah's mother Paulina and stepfather George
Southwick had four children, Mary Anne, Henry, Cornelia and
Augusta, born between 1816 and 1826.

In 1830, Hannah Howard married Solomon Jennings (1802-1881). Not much is known about her husband, except that his parents were John Jennings and Elizabeth Clark, from Vermont. Hannah may have met him while she was away at school, or visiting relatives in New York or Rhode Island. Whether Solomon's parents had been Quakers or not, he joined a meeting before their marriage, which may have taken place before they settled in Upper Canada. They made their home on part of George Southwick's land, where Solomon worked as a farmer, later becoming an owner. (He was assessed for Lot 4, the east portion of the Southwick land, in 1845.)[10] Norwich Township had an abundance of fine land. In the area where the Jennings lived, it was for the most part a fertile sandy loam, and, as Peter Lossing had reported two decades earlier, it offered a reward for the harsh toil of pioneering. At the time of Hannah's marriage to Solomon Jennings, a township was mainly a division of land. A number of townships made up the county, which was the electoral unit. The district, usually larger than any county, was the unit of local government, where, at the call of the magistrates, a town meeting could be held to deal with local issues, which were numerous.

The period of the 1830s was characterized by dissent in certain quarters of Upper Canada. While the majority of the populace was apolitical and preoccupied with the struggle to survive in the forest clearings, a minority felt frustrated that their elected representatives in the legislature at Muddy York were politically impotent. Real power lay with the lieutenant-governor, appointed by the British government, and with the legislative and executive councils of men who were appointed for life. Opinion in the province was divided into two main factions: Tories, who had the ear of the lieutenant-governor, and Reformers, who sought a means of making the government responsible to the elected members of the legislature. The Lossing men were nearly all Reformers, and Solomon Jennings sided with them.

As time passed, seven children were born to Hannah and Solomon Jennings; the eldest was to be the first Canadian woman doctor:

Emily Howard Jennings, 1 May, 1831

Cornelia Lossing Jennings, 8 January, 1835

Paulina Jennings, 10 May, 1838

Ethelinda Jennings, 25 October, 1841

John Milton Jennings, 22 April, 1844, died 23 September, 1844

Hannah Augusta Jennings, 30 April, 1846

Ella Jennings, 23 September, 1848[11]

For both parents the loss of their only son remained a constant heartache. However, because of their Quaker background, they placed as great value on daughters as on sons. Amongst Quakers, women shared equally with men in the conduct of their meetings and in every other aspect of daily life. The Quaker understanding of equality was well expressed many years later by William Greenwood Brown, a member of the Toronto Central Meeting of Friends:

> The general attitude of the Quaker is that the State should be modelled after the constitution and the spirit of the home; that the husband and wife have a partnership voice in the government of the home, in the Church (so far as Quakers are concerned) and should have in the State.[12]

The Quaker setting contributed to the six daughters' determination to extend that equality beyond the meeting house and the Quaker-oriented home. Equality was instilled as well through the education Hannah Jennings gave her daughters; it took precedence over the demand of work on the rudimentary farm. These demands were considerable. With no boys in the family, necessity ruled that the Jennings girls help out with the heavier tasks on the land, as well as with work about the house. The days started early, with milking the cows, and they found no relief until after dark. The nature of the work depended on the season. Nearly everything the family needed was made at home — clothing, most of the furniture, soap and candles. During the growing season, foods had to be preserved to tide the Jennings over the winter; they bottled fruits and vegetables, dried apples, stored potatoes and carrots in a root cellar and flour in barrels. Before the snow came, the loft of the barn had to be piled high with hay, and the bins filled with grain for the livestock. Norwich Township was still a primitive place at the time of Emily's birth.

In 1818, Solomon Lossing, then the township clerk, had filled in the questionnaire circulated by the Scottish radical reformer, Robert Gourlay. Lossing stated that Norwich had two Quaker meeting houses, three schools, one store, one grist mill (two others were under construction) and three saw mills. The very first school in the southern half of the township was said to have been kept in his own home by Emily's step-grandfather, George Southwick.[13] The Jennings girls were not sent to any of the schools because Hannah disapproved of them. In 1830, Dr. Charles Duncombe, a Reform Party member of the Upper Canadian Assembly representing Oxford County, chaired a select committee on schools. The committee reported that the common schools were in deplorable condition.[14] Hannah Howard Jennings was better qualified to impart knowledge than most teachers in the schools of the day.

Medical practice, too, was in a backward state. Throughout Upper Canada medical practitioners were very few, and opportunities to become qualified were almost non-existent. Nevertheless, by statutes of 1795, 1815, 1818 and 1819, unqualified persons were forbidden to practise, and an examining board functioned. Some men from the neighbourhood attended medical classes at the Fairfield Academy, in Herkimer County, New York, and after study for as little as sixteen weeks, returned and obtained licences to practise from the Upper Canada Medical Board. Among them were Elijah Eli and David, younger brothers of Dr. Charles Duncombe, the Member of the Legislature. Dr. Duncombe and another physician, English-born Dr. John Rolph, opened medical classes in St. Thomas in 1824. Although both Reformers, they named their establishment the Talbot Dispensary, to flatter Colonel Thomas Talbot, the crusty arch-Tory whose word was law in the settlement. Duncombe and Rolph also dispensed medicines for the poor. The first attempt at a medical school in the province was short-lived, and Rolph soon moved to the town of Dundas.[15]

Many people were treated at home by women. Like most frontier wives and mothers, Hannah Howard Jennings had a vast knowledge of herbal remedies. Pioneer settlements had a long tradition of woman healers, and attendance at birth was usually a woman's business. Growing up among healers like her mother undoubtedly convinced Emily that women naturally made good practitioners. Some women were so active caring for the sick that they were thought to have been doctors. One such was Mrs. Lydia Trull, who arrived at Niagara from

New York State with her husband, John, in 1794. The Trulls were among the first settlers in Darlington Township, Durham County. Lydia's descendants treasured an iron pot in which she mixed her herbal medicines. She brought with her a book on midwifery and healing of the sick. She rode horseback through the forest along blazed trails, and forded rushing rivers to be at the side of her patients.[16] Emily could recall her mother going out to attend someone who was ill, or being summoned to a "lying in," a euphemism for childbirth.

At the same time, many unlicensed male practitioners, ignoring the statutes, flourished as herb-doctors. Samuel Thomson's *New Guide to Health or Botanic Physician* was widely used in the community. A Canadian edition was published in Hamilton in 1832. Thomson was a poorly educated New Hampshire farmer who began treating patients with medicines derived from plants — a botanic as opposed to a traditional practitioner who treated with mineral-based drugs and bleeding. Using the book, one supposedly became one's own physician.[17]

Methodists believed in the medical work of John Wesley, founder of their faith, whose book, *Primitive Physic or an Easy Natural Method of Curing Most Diseases*, was first published in 1747.[18] Thomson and Wesley both had recommendations for coping with fever and ague (malaria). Thomson viewed fever as a friend, and wrote, "when the fever fit is on, increase the power of heat in order to drive off the cold." Wesley wrote, "Nothing tends more to prolong an ague than indulging a lazy, indolent disposition ... the patient ought ... between the fits ... to take as much exercise as he can bear ... [and] use a light diet ....[F]or common drink, Port Wine and water is most proper."[19]

A myriad variety of plants and minerals was used, while self-dosing with patent medicines containing undisclosed ingredients was widespread. Many consisted of strong narcotics (laudanum — tincture of opium — was popular) which temporarily made a patient feel better. Alcoholism was a danger from the use of patent medicines, for many were little more than high proof spirits.[20] Edward Jenner had published the effects of inoculation with cowpox vaccine to immunize against smallpox in 1798, but his work was not yet generally accepted although smallpox epidemics were not uncommon. In Norwich, home remedies were the most favoured, even after the arrival of the township's first doctor, Ephraim Cook, who settled at Sodom, the main village, in 1830.[21] (Quakers named the community Sodom because in the village stood that fount of all evils, a tavern.) The first to set up practice closer to the Jennings home was George Washington Carter. He came from New York State in 1836, and opened his office in Otterville, the nearest village to the land of Emily's family.[22] By that time Norwich was more preoccupied with secure land titles and political reform than with health care.

Even before Emily's birth, Norwich had been in an uproar over land problems. The government had sold the township to speculators to raise money to extend Dundas Street eastwards from York. The first surveys, in 1799, had been poorly carried out. They led to endless boundary quarrels. In 1834, the legislature, in which a majority of the members were Reformers, set up a committee to investigate the matter. This was also chaired by Dr. Charles Duncombe, by then the leading Reformer in Oxford County. English-born John Arthur Tidey was hired to resurvey the township, but many residents were still not satisfied. Farmers barricaded new road construction with fencing, and tore out surveyors' stakes wherever they thought they would be deprived of land they believed they owned.

Most of the Norwich Quakers were Reformers, led by Emily's great-uncle, Solomon Lossing, a magistrate as well as a respected farmer on Lots 1 and 2, Concession 7, with saw and grist mills along the Otter Creek. Solomon, who presided with other magistrates over the Courts of Quarter Sessions, was known to all as "Squire Lossing." He was a staunch believer in the need for change because of the state of the surveys in Norwich. From his Quaker view it was important to separate church and state and to provide adequate schools in Upper Canada. The people of Norwich were Baptists and Methodists, as well as Quakers. Anglicans constituted only a tiny minority. The other residents objected to the endowment of some forty Church of England rectories in the area by Lieutenant-Governor Sir John Colborne. This was correctly seen as a blatant attempt to create an established church.[23]

The year 1836, when a precociously bright Emily Jennings was five years old, was a dark one for the Reformers of Norwich. A new lieutenant-governor, Sir Francis Bond Head, called an election which threw out the Reform majority and brought in a Tory administration. For William Lyon Mackenzie, the leader of the radical Reformers around the capital, now renamed Toronto, this meant rebellion. Dr. Charles Duncombe, equally disgruntled, was prepared to lead a rising in the London District. The opposition to the Reformers was on hand in the person of William Brearley, who had settled on Lot 21, Concession 6 in Norwich. An Englishman and high Tory, Brearley was the acting lieutenant-colonel of the 1st Oxford Regiment of Militia (his commission was not signed until the eighth of February, 1838). Brearley, one of the few Anglicans in Norwich, was surrounded by an overwhelming majority of Nonconformists. Not only that, but Brearley was a newcomer who had arrived in the township in 1836. Reformers like Squire Lossing and government supporters like Colonel Brearley were at daggers-drawn by 1837.

The events of 1837 and 1838 and later, are vital to an understanding of the character of Emily Howard Jennings, the future Dr. Stowe. They conditioned her stubborn response to the seemingly insurmountable obstacles to her acquiring a medical education. Even after she had qualified, she had to overcome further impediments to the practice of medicine by a woman.

TWO

Regina versus Lossing

BY THE AUTUMN OF 1837, William Lyon Mackenzie was touring the Home District, organizing political unions, and advocating the capture of Toronto. His was to be a bloodless coup to induce the British government to take seriously the need for reform. Dr. Charles Duncombe was in much the same frame of mind, for, as President of the Constitutional Reform Society, he had taken a list of complaints to England in 1836. He returned disillusioned, and began to organize political union meetings in the London District. Mackenzie was present at some of them. On the second of September,1837, a meeting was held in Daniel Bedford's inn at Sodom (now Norwich village). Reformers in both the Home and London Districts planned a convention and demonstration in Toronto for the spring of 1838. John Arthur Tidey and Peter DeLong agreed to be delegates to the convention.[1] At the time, Emily's great-uncle, Solomon Lossing, while recognized as the leader among the Reformers in Norwich, was keeping a low profile, but there must have been much discussion of the situation in the Jennings household.

On the eighth of December, rebels robbed William Cromwell's store in Otterville of powder, shot, cloth, tea and tobacco.[2] Robbery was such an unusual event that it would have incited much comment in the Jennings farmhouse. The same day or the next, a group of Reformers met at Sodom, among them Solomon Lossing, and Dr.

Duncombe arrived from his home at Bishopsgate in Burford Township to address them. Duncombe reported that Mackenzie had besieged Toronto with from three to four thousand men. The next day, some two to three hundred attended a public meeting at Sodom, where Duncombe claimed that Mackenzie had been successful. He urged the men to follow him to attack Brantford where too many Tories lived, and he offered each volunteer 100 acres and twelve dollars a month. About eighty signed up; one was Peter DeLong's son, Garrett. John Treffry, the husband of Mary Anne Southwick, Solomon Lossing's niece and Emily's aunt, stuck to his Quaker pacifist principles and refused to let the intended rebels have his rifle.[3] Solomon Lossing was seen with the rebels and was reported to have been encouraging them.[4] Solomon Jennings may have been among the men who listened to Duncombe but, like John Treffry, his Quaker principles — or at least concern for his young family — kept him from further participation.

On the twelfth, Duncombe left Norwich with 200 men — 54 of them actually from Norwich — bound for Scotland, a village near the eastern boundary of Burford Township, where the rebels were to muster for an attack on Brantford. At Scotland the next day Duncombe's band learned that Mackenzie had not taken Toronto, and that a large body of volunteers loyal to the government had ridden into Brantford. They were led by the owner of Hamilton's Dundurn Castle, Colonel Allan MacNab, of the Gore District Militia. Most of MacNab's volunteers were drawn from the Gore regiments, men who had flocked into Hamilton, the district seat, eager to follow the colonel. At the same time as MacNab and his volunteers were leaving Brantford, Duncombe's rebels were melting back into Norwich Township looking for refuge in sympathetic homes, while their demoralized leader was fleeing to the safety of the United States.

Now Emily's great-uncle became embroiled, and not too willingly. One of the rebels, Elias Snider, came to Harmon Sprague's farm in East Oxford Township and asked him to go to MacNab to enquire whether the rebels could surrender without reprisals. Sprague sought the counsel of Solomon Lossing who, after hesitating, agreed to act as a go-between. On the fourteenth, MacNab was in Scotland. Lossing arrived with a deputation of three — himself, Peter Sackrider and the Otterville merchant, William Cromwell. They approached MacNab and asked under what terms the rebels might give themselves up. MacNab said he would do all he could to see that the authorities took no action. Lossing, aware that MacNab had at least 800 armed men with him and that more were converging on Scotland, returned to Sodom and persuaded many rebels to surrender.

By the sixteenth of December, a Saturday, MacNab had a thousand men scouring Norwich, but most of the ringleaders among the rebels had fled. The militia commander set up three posts, one in the north at Burgessville, another at centrally located Sodom, and the third in the south, close to Emily's home, at William Cromwell's mill and store in Otterville. Colonel William Brearley was in command of this post; he set up a jail in the store. On the seventeenth, Solomon Lossing and some 200 Norwich men assembled at Sodom. They were quickly surrounded by rows of militia from other parts of the London and Gore districts. The Norwich men handed MacNab a petition with 103 names on it, asking for mercy because Duncombe had betrayed them. MacNab agreed to send their petition to Lieutenant Governor Head. MacNab then lectured the men and allowed all to go home, except Solomon Lossing.

As a magistrate, Lossing had a duty to report all treasonable plans. MacNab accused him of supplying the rebels with pork and with flour from his mill. Because Squire Lossing had been present at most of Duncombe's meetings, MacNab arrested him in front of the many men gathered at Sodom.[5] News that Emily's great uncle had been escorted from Sodom to the jail in Hamilton horrified her closer relatives. Jail was for criminals, not respectable folk like the Lossings. Possibly her own father had been among the men listening to MacNab's harangue at Sodom and had witnessed the arrest of his relative. (According to the family, Solomon Lossing was held in Dundurn Castle, but no record suggests that MacNab or any other authority treated a suspected rebel with such consideration.)

Even Emily, a child of six, could not be shielded from the events that followed the arrest of Solomon Lossing. A vindictive militia searched for stray rebels throughout Norwich. The citizen-soldiers also looked for weapons and ammunition to disarm the township. MacNab's army required billets and meals which had to be obtained from the local populace since his force had travelled light and with speed. He had neither a commissariat officer nor the supplies to sustain a force now numbered at more than a thousand men. Since they were relatives of Solomon Lossing, the Jennings' home may have been searched repeatedly. Though no record survives for the Jennings household, the adventures of Emily's maternal grandmother, Paulina Lossing Howard Southwick, who lived almost next door, were written down and have been preserved.

Paulina and her second husband, George Southwick, hid a rebel named LaPhaette Barnes who came seeking refuge. Paulina had a bed curtain hung to hide a door that led to another room where she left Barnes. When the militia arrived, she told their officer, "Come in and look for yourself." They did not find Barnes, but after they left she told him, "Come Phaette thee must go elsewhere." Her husband took two horses and accompanied Barnes for some distance, then returned with the horses while Barnes continued on foot, presumably towards the border and the safety of the United States.[6]

Horror stories circulated about the abuses of the militia and of the terror spread by the mere sight of the Indian warriors who accompanied them. Oliver Jaques, seven years old at the time, remembered Indians invading the kitchen and putting on their war paint before a mirror. Afterwards, they threw their hatchets against trees and disappeared into the woods.[7] Residents hid their wagons and horses so that the militia could not requisition them, and concealed food to sustain themselves until the crops of 1838 were ready to harvest.

Many other rebels slipped out of Norwich and made for the United States. Among them were Dr. Ephraim Cook and a farmer of Quaker background named Joseph Lancaster, whose land lay north of Sodom. One of Duncombe's ensigns, Lancaster was jailed, but released on bail soon afterwards as a reward for betraying other insurgents. He was later accused of being a rebel hunter. He forfeited bail and fled to the United States, to avoid further questioning. (In later years he would be a good friend to Emily, and help her in her medical career).[8]

Meanwhile, Solomon Lossing lay in Hamilton jail, accused of condoning the rebels' having thirty to forty "stand of arms" at a Norwich political union meeting. Peter DeLong, aged sixty, was indicted on the ninth of April, 1838, but he was temporarily in the United States. His son, Garrett, jailed in Hamilton from the twenty-third of December, was paroled a month later, after which he, too, left the country. The surveyor, John Arthur Tidey, aged thirty-eight, appointed secretary to the rebel movement by Dr. Duncombe, was in jail in London.

By that time, Norwich was no longer part of the London District. The District of Brock had been created in 1837 by an act of the legislature, with Woodstock as the district seat. The area within the new district comprised all of Oxford County and part of Brant. By early 1838, Brock had not begun to function, and Woodstock had neither a courthouse nor a jail. Confinements and trials took place in Hamilton and London since these district seats had the necessary facilities.

Solomon Lossing's trial, before Judge James Buchanan Macaulay, was scheduled to begin on Monday, the second of April, 1838, with Emily's father, Solomon Jennings, as a key witness. When Jennings — for no known reason — failed to appear at the Hamilton Court House, the trial was postponed to the next day. Even then Solomon Jennings' name was not among the witnesses for the defence. There were nine witnesses, including Mary Anne Treffry, Emily's aunt and governess to some of Solomon Lossing's children. Of the nine Crown witnesses, two were Lossing's sons, Augustus and Albert, and Andrew Drew, the half-pay naval officer who had led the party that destroyed the American steamship *Caroline* on the twenty-ninth of December, 1837, which caused an international incident deeply embarrassing to Britain.[9] Meanwhile, the Jennings family waited anxiously for news from Hamilton. Conditions in the jail were so poor that a lengthy confinement could damage any man's health, and Emily's great uncle was fifty-four at that time.

The indictment against Solomon Lossing was very serious, because of his standing in the township as a justice of the peace. He was charged with high treason:

First Count — conspiring the Queen's death
  — overt acts laid
  — furnishing provisions to rebels

Second Count — levying war against the Queen

Lossing's lawyers were of good repute: James McGill Strachan, the eldest son of the Reverend John Strachan, soon to be the first bishop of Toronto, and Hamilton R. O'Reilly (who was with Andrew Drew at the cutting out of the *Caroline*). The Crown presented evidence that Lossing had given flour freely to the rebels. The question was raised as to why Lossing had not attempted to arrest Duncombe (which would have been nearly impossible among so many sympathizers.) However, a friendly jury brought in a verdict of "Not Guilty" and Emily's great uncle was free to leave the discomforts of the cold, evil-smelling jail and return home to Norwich. He was released on the twenty-third of April, 1838.[10] The government did not deprive him of his appointment as justice of the peace, but for the moment Lossing had lost considerable standing in his community.

Tensions in Norwich did not abate; the fear generated by these events affected the young as well as their older relatives. As summer approached, Colonel Brearley was sending to Toronto messages of secret meetings and a threatening atmosphere. The people of Norwich were in frequent communication with Canadian exiles now gathered in Lockport, New York, and agents were slipping into the township. Loyal residents asked for a detachment of militia to be stationed in Norwich. In June, Canadian exiles and American sympathizers staged a raid into the Short Hills, in the Niagara Peninsula. After the invaders had been put to flight, some rebels and their American guests made their escape into Norwich where they hoped to find friends to shelter them. By July all of Oxford County was in fear of terrorist acts, inspired by the many secret meetings, oaths and passwords, and rumours of a large-scale uprising planned for the fourth or fifth of July. No rising occurred, but on the fourth a band of insurgents burned Colonel Brearley's house to the ground.[11]

Rebel prisoners were again confined in William Cromwell's store in Otterville until they could be conveyed to Hamilton or London. Once again militia from other parts of the district arrived in Norwich to keep the peace, and again the citizen-soldiers imposed on the residents for billets and food. On the sixth of July, Solomon Lossing and his sons, twenty-year-old William and seventeen-year-old Horace, were arrested. Solomon and William were released after half-an-hour, but Horace was held longer on suspicion of having taken the oath of a secret society in Norwich. He was sent to Hamilton, and by the early autumn he was moved to London before he received clemency. Solomon complained to the new governor-general, Lord Durham, that militia officers took his seven-year-old son hostage until he, Solomon, could surrender a rifle. As the rifle was not at the house, the lad was marched three miles to be locked in a military guardroom. There the child remained until the distraught Solomon recovered the rifle the next day and handed it to Colonel Brearley.[12]

An unsigned petition, dated the fifteenth of July, 1838, was sent to Sir Francis Bond Head's successor, Lieutenant Governor Sir George Arthur, protesting the abuses by the militia and citing an incident at which Emily may well have been present:

> They went to the Quaker Meeting house during the hours of
> worship watched their coming out and turned feeble women
> and young children out of their waggons 3 and 4 miles from
> their homes and took their teams for the purpose of convey-
> ing the Indians without any baggage the distance of 6 miles
> but the   Indians being more humane chose to walk and the
> teams were suffered to follow their owners home .... [13]

In early August, Solomon Lossing sent a petition with twenty-five signatures to Governor Arthur complaining about other abuses by the militia.[14] Emily, the eldest daughter, precocious and mature for her years, must have been aware of most of what was going on around her. If Great-uncle Solomon was not intimidated by all he had been put through, nor would she be when her time came.

In December, when the authorities released Horace Lossing from jail in London, Canadian exiles and their American supporters staged a bloody raid on Windsor. Two well-known Norwich men, Paul and Daniel Bedford, were captured at Windsor and taken to the London jail. For his part, Paul was sentenced to fourteen years' transportation to the notorious penal colony on Van Diemen's Land (Tasmania); he was later freed in London, England. Daniel was sentenced to death, and was hanged in London, Upper Canada, on the eleventh of January, 1839.[15] The execution shocked the people of Norwich, young and old, who turned out for the burial in the Friends' cemetery after Daniel's father brought the body home.

As the months passed tensions abated and gradually the rebels were forgiven. Dr. Ephraim Cook was soon back in Sodom, practising medicine and living quietly. The DeLongs returned to Norwich where Peter died on the twenty-sixth of June, 1839. (Peter Lossing, Emily's great grandfather, and DeLong were founders of the Quaker settlement.) John Arthur Tidey took the initiative, in January, 1840, and wrote a petition to the governor, now Charles Poulett Thomson. (As Lord Sydenham, in 1841, Thomson would be the first Governor of the United Province of Canada.) The petition stated that Colonel Brearley, who had come to live in Norwich Township four years before, and who had received several appointments, had been the cause of many complaints. Tidey asked for an enquiry into Brearley's conduct.[16] Later, Brearley was removed as a magistrate and he resigned his commission in the militia when the government placed no more confidence in his abilities. The same year he ended his public career and moved to Port Burwell.[17] Those who had rebelled, however, were gradually forgiven, and many who had gone into exile returned home. Great-uncle Solomon was soon back in favour.

To Emily Howard Jennings, growing older and understanding these events around her, the lesson was clear. Persistence and standing up to intimidation paid off. In the long run, the Reformers were the victors. Many of the changes they had sought came about. In the meantime, Upper and Lower Canada were united under one Parliament in 1841, the year Emily turned ten. Now she had to remember that the province where she lived had been renamed Canada West. Responsible government was granted when Governor-General Lord Elgin arrived in 1847 with orders to affix the Royal assent to any measure passed by Parliament. The Reformers had triumphed, while William Brearley, the high-handed Tory, had been run out of Norwich Township.

THREE

First Woman Principal

THE HAMLET OF SUMMERVILLE LIES some two miles from the site of the Jennings home in South Norwich. In 1846, the little log schoolhouse at Summerville lacked a teacher. According to John Treffry, Emily's uncle, the log building was near her Great-uncle Benson Lossing's home at Summerville.[1] By a School Act of 1843, each county had a Superintendent of Education, and under him each township had a superintendent. Reverend N. Bosworth was the superintendent for Oxford, and Dr. Ephraim Cook for Norwich.[2] Both were lay appointees; later, positions would be filled by professional educators. Casting about for a teacher for Summerville, Dr. Cook chose fifteen-year-old Emily Jennings, although taught at home, as the best qualified person available. Delighted with this golden opportunity to earn her own living, Emily threw herself enthusiastically into teaching the local young people.

In their one-room school, Emily's pupils came in all sizes and ages, whenever they were not needed for farm or house work at home. Some of the boys were bigger than their teacher, but Emily had no difficulty with them. She could be forceful without being overbearing. The work load was heavy, as she had to prepare lessons for many different levels and check all the pupils' work.

Some time between 1845 and 1851, Emily's family moved from the farm into Sodom village (which people were beginning to call

Norwichville, although legally the more unfortunate name still applied). Solomon Jennings was bailiff for the village, under the district sheriff. The rehabilitated Solomon Lossing was the Warden for the District of Brock in the 1840s and may have had a hand in Jennings's appointment. The census of 1851 recorded that Jennings, aged fifty, had a one and a half storey frame house on Lot 4, Concession 11. His wife Hannah was then forty-three. The daughters were listed as Emily, twenty, Cornelia, eighteen, Paulina, fourteen, "Catherine" (Ethelinda), ten, Hannah, six, and "Emma" (Ella), three. Other township records show that Solomon Jennings bought and sold land frequently. He was able to make a living from his appointment and his land transactions and had given up farming. Meanwhile, Emily continued teaching school, but not in Summerville. Records for the District of Brock, 1848, show that she was teaching in School Section One. In 1849 and 1850 the school records for Oxford County (that had replaced the district as the administrative unit) showed that she was teaching in Burgessville, in School Section Four. Salaries for women teachers varied from £21 with board up to £37.15.0 without board. Male teachers received as much as £59.0.2 without board, and £47.3.4 with board.[3]

Emily taught school for about seven years. Evidently Dr. Cook was satisfied with her. By the time she was twenty-two she was thirsting for more education for herself. She applied for admission to Victoria College in Cobourg, but she was refused on grounds that women were not eligible. This was particularly galling to a Quaker. Since 1841 the Quakers had been operating the West Lake Boarding School in Prince Edward County, and like all such Quaker institutions, it was co-educational.[4]

However, one form of higher education available to women was preparation for teaching. Women teachers were becoming popular with school trustees because they did not have to be paid as much as men, the erroneous assumption being that a man had a family to support while a woman had only herself. The School Act of 1846 had provided for a provincial Superintendent of Education and for a Normal School where teachers could be trained. By 1853 the superintendent was Dr. Egerton Ryerson, the Methodist preacher.[5] With money saved from her years of teaching in Norwich, Emily took herself off to the Provincial Normal School in Toronto in November 1853, a brave venture for a country-bred young woman conspicuous in the plain dress of a Quaker.

Toronto must have seemed an alien world to Emily. With a population of more than 25,000, it appeared to be so cosmopolitan. As yet, Toronto had no Quaker meeting but she found many Methodists and Baptists, the other two denominations so familiar to her in Norwich. The power of the Anglican establishment, however, was new to her. She soon found that the two dominant personalities in the city were the Anglican Bishop John Strachan and the Methodist, Dr. Egerton Ryerson. Their mutual dislike was so strong that the one would cross the street if he noticed the approach of the other.

The Provincial Normal School was very new and grand — the cornerstone had been laid in July 1851 by Governor-General Lord Elgin. The awesome edifice stood at Gerrard and Church Streets (the present site of Ryerson Polytechnic Institute). The headmaster was Thomas J. Robertson, whom Dr. Ryerson had hired in Dublin while he was visiting the city to study the Dublin Normal School.[6] Emily was allowed free books and tuition, and one dollar a week towards her board — in an approved house. Curfew was 9.00 p.m. and male students were not allowed to speak to females at school, or meet outside it.[7] This may have been Emily's first experience of strict segregation, so different from the easy interchanges between the sexes at home. In the Model School, which stood behind the main building and was reached by a corridor, one side was assigned to the girls, the other to the boys. This elementary school served the Normal School as a place for practice teaching.[8] Despite the affront of segregation, Emily resolved to make the best of her situation, however much she disapproved. She had come to Toronto so that she could command a higher salary, and she had enough confidence in her own ability to know that she would do well academically.

The teacher training course lasted for six months.[9] Already experienced, Emily started in November, sailed through the programme and graduated in May, 1854, with First Class Honours. Her record so impressed the chairman of the Brantford School Board, James Wilkes, and his fellow trustees, that they hired her as the principal of their oldest public school (later the Brantford Central School).[10] Miss Emily Jennings was the first woman to be appointed principal of a public school in Ontario (still known as Canada West in 1854).

Her diploma was signed on the third of April, 1854, by Dr. Thomas Robertson, Headmaster, and William Ormiston, A.B., second master. Her first class certificate dated twentieth of April 1854, and signed by Dr. Egerton Ryerson, was attached to it. Emily's grandson, Hudson Stowe, made copies and presented the original certificate to the Ryerson Polytechnical Institute because it was built on the site of the old Provincial Normal School.

Once the appointment was secure, Emily faced the sad task of parting with her fellow student teachers. Many composed poems in her honour which she stored carefully in a special brown leather album. They suggest that despite social restrictions, male and female students became very close friends. Alfred E. Ecroyd wrote, with a split infinitive that surely would have distressed their English teacher:

> May you thrice happy be
> But oh! mid all your future joys
> To kindly think of *me*.

Another of similar sentiment was signed by Francis W. Bird. Even the assistant headmaster, William Ormiston, was devoted to Emily. Scottish-born Ormiston, who taught mathematics and chemistry, was a Presbyterian minister. He was appointed to St. James Square United Presbyterian Church in 1853, the year he came to teach at the Normal school. Ormiston wrote to Emily on the eighteenth of March, 1854

> May you never be without a God, without a *friend*, without a
> *hope*, without a *home*, and when your soul is weary of the joys
> of earth may it rise to the glories of Heaven, and there may
> you meet your teacher. [11]

With her keepsake album and other possessions, Emily set out to spend the summer at home. She left for her new posting in September.

The Brantford school had been founded in 1826 in a log building that also served as a meeting hall and a church. When Emily arrived in 1854 it was housed in a brick building that had been opened by Dr. Ryerson in 1850. (This became the west wing of Brantford Central School; the centre block was added in 1857 and the east wing in 1871.)

Brantford also had a grammar school, opened in 1852, in a small frame cottage that had previously housed a private school.

She taught for two years until her marriage in Norwichville on the twenty-second of November, 1856, to John Stowe.[12] John's home was at Mount Pleasant, a village about five miles south of Brantford. As was the custom, she resigned when she married. Yet she had no regrets, for as she wrote later, "I believe homemaking, of all occupations that fall to woman's lot, the one most important and far reaching in its effects upon humanity."[13]

The Stowes were Methodists from Yorkshire, England. John Stowe was thirteen when his parents brought him to Mount Pleasant in 1843. John's father, John Stowe Sr., was a tailor. He arranged for his two brothers-in-law, to build him an octagonal house to shelter his family and business. Downstairs was his shop, while the family's living quarters were on the upper storey. With his younger brother, William, John Jr. started a carriage-making business. Together they built a second octagonal house, which still stands, for young John's bride.[14] Downstairs was the carriage shop, with a blacksmith's shop at the rear. Like his parents, John and Emily would make their home in the upper storey.

As a staunch Methodist, John Stowe probably did not want a Quaker ceremony, and they may have been married by the Methodist minister of Norwichville. A couple married themselves among Friends, since they believed that no mediator was necessary. The bride and groom simply spoke their vows at the monthly meeting, promising to be true to each other until death. The marriage certificate was signed in the presence of the meeting by the couple, parents and close relatives, and preserved with the other records of the congregation.[15] Quakers traditionally disowned members of the meeting who failed to marry according to set practices, but an exception seems to have been made with the Jennings family. Emily's first child, Ann Augusta, was born in Norwich on the twenty-seventh of July, 1857.[16] Like most young women, Emily went to her mother's for her first "lying in."

Emily had settled down very happily, content with her role as wife and mother. As time passed she dressed less and less like a Quaker. She attended Methodist services, as much because John wanted her at his side as from conviction. In 1859 John became a lay preacher in the circuit to which their Mount Pleasant chapel belonged.[17] A son, John Howard, was born on the tenth of February, 1861, at Mount Pleasant. Their second son, Frank Jennings, born on the twenty-fourth of August, 1863, completed the family. By the time of Frank's birth, their father's health was failing from pulmonary tuberculosis, the most common cause of death at that time.[18]

Emily's attitude to disease may well have been the saving of her husband. Her mother was well known for the remedies she prepared from roots and herbs, and she passed her knowledge on to her eldest daughter. Both women leaned towards the homeopathic practice of medicine, and the person who indoctrinated them might have been Joseph J. Lancaster (1813-1884), the native of Norwich and old friend of the Jennings family. Lancaster was the first homeopathic practitioner in Ontario.[19] The doctrine of Samuel Thomson, that every man was his own physician, had lost popularity soon after Thomson's death in 1843, and homeopathy — and other practices that bordered on the faddish — were gradually replacing it. Lancaster, who had farmed eighty acres near Sodom, was one of Dr. Charles Duncombe's rebels who had been imprisoned in London. After he had been released on bail he fled to the United States and studied medicine at a homeopathic college. Upon his return to Canada he practised for a while in Norwich, moving to London in 1848.[20]

Homeopathy was a doctrine expounded towards the close of the eighteenth century by Samuel Hahnemann of Meissen, Germany. He found that Peruvian bark (from which quinine was extracted) could produce the symptoms of malaria in a healthy person. He concluded that was the reason why patients with malaria became well after treatment with quinine. Next, he proceeded to the conclusion that infinitesimal quantites of a drug were more effective than large doses. Even some physicians whose training had been orthodox were turning towards homeopathy because the usual treatments — bleeding, purges, clysters (enemas) and mineral waters — were ineffective.[21] The tiny doses Hahnemann advocated did little good, but they allowed nature to take its course undisturbed, saving a patient from drastic if orthodox treatment that often hastened death.[22]

As well as homeopathics, there were eclectics and hydropathics. Eclectics, or Botanics, used only natural medicines, rejecting those containing chemicals and minerals, but even then they were selective. Hydropaths believed in using only water as cures, externally and internally. The first spa in Upper Canada opened at Caledonia Springs in 1836. The springs were south of the Ottawa River near L'Original. Other spas existed at Kingston and Ancaster. By the 1850s hydropathy was branded as quackery.[23] Homeopathy was more acceptable, and the distinctions between homeopathics and orthodox practitioners and eclectics were often blurred. In 1850, Dr. Joseph Lancaster petitioned the legislative assembly for homeopaths to be allowed to practise in Canada West. The assembly passed "An Act Respecting Homeopathy" in 1859, which appointed a board of examiners to license homeopathic physicians.[24] Restraint in the use of "heroic" drugs, as those prescribed by regular physicians were called, could have contributed to John Stowe's survival.

According to family lore, John went to a sanatorium to recover, which is no doubt how his children explained his absence. However, the sanatorium movement was in its infancy in the 1860s. The first sanatorium in North America was opened in 1884 at Saranac Lake by the New York physician Dr. Edward Trudeau. Himself a victim of tuberculosis, Trudeau found that he recovered his health by living as much as possible in the open air of the Adirondack Mountains.[25]

Emily must have suspected that John could pass the disease on to the children, and that they had to be protected from close contact with him. Exactly where John was treated is not known. Some physicians cared for patients in their own homes, or operated small private nursing homes, but few records of these establishments survive. Possibly Dr. Joseph Lancaster, who was well known to Emily at the time, was one who believed in the virtues of plenty of rest and fresh air.[26]

The proposition that a patient with pulmonary tuberculosis should spend most of the time in the open air was articulated in 1840 by Dr. George Bodington, of Sutton Coldfield, England, in his *Essay on the Treatment and Cure of Pulmonary Consumption.* His article was not well received; the British medical journal *Lancet* ridiculed the notion in the June, 1840, issue. Bodington, undaunted, went ahead and opened a house near his home where patients could receive fresh air, exercise and nutritious food in contrast to the recommendation of many physicians — dark, closed rooms and starvation diets, all to the detriment of their patients. When Bodington died in 1882, *Lancet* published an obituary praising him for being ahead of his time.[27] In the Ontario of the 1860s, only an *avant-garde* physician would have advocated fresh air and good food, and possibly gentle exercise. Emily had somehow found the right treatment for her husband.

Emily was now faced with the necessity of supporting the family. The Nelles Academy at Mount Pleasant was founded in 1846 by the Stowes' friend, Dr. William Waggoner Nelles, as a private school for young men. Nelles was the headmaster and a brother of Reverend Samuel Nelles, the President of Victoria College in Cobourg. Dr. Nelles leased the land from the wealthy early settler, Abraham Cooke. The Nelles Academy building was octagonal, like the Stowe houses, and it, too, may have been the work of John Stowe's brothers-in-law. The academy building with its land had been sold in 1860 by Mr. Cooke, but it became the County Grammar School soon afterwards and Dr. Nelles remained as the principal. Aware of Emily's predicament, he offered her a place on his staff which she gratefully accepted. The pay was poor, but it was the best available at that time without uprooting the family. She embarked upon a busy round of teaching, preparing lessons, marking work, and caring for three young children. For many women, but not for Emily Stowe, domestic life would have been demanding enough without the addition of professional responsibility, at least until such time as John had recovered and could support his family again.[28]

She had resolved to become a doctor, and as soon as possible. When her other work was done and the children were asleep, she began studying to prepare for college entrance examinations. Women, she protested, ought to be doctors; they were fitted for the role by nature. In the past, and especially in a frontier community such as Norwich Township, women had looked after the health of their families as a matter of course. Once a community had enough men trained as physicians they usurped woman's traditional role. For generations women had had a place in health care, especially as midwives; physician, surgeon and apothecary were separate professions. Early in the nineteenth century, physician and apothecary became one, and by Emily's time all doctors were general practitioners who performed surgery.[29]

Women, Emily realized, were being short changed by the general practitioners who were, without exception, male. "Respectable" modest women were unwilling to discuss intimate matters with a man, or subject their bodies to examination. Emily was determined to help fill the need of the female population. She was loyally supported by her family in her resolve, especially by her sister Cornelia who had married a fellow-Quaker, David Benjamin Kelso, in 1856. Cornelia agreed to move into the Mount Pleasant house and care for her niece and nephews, who were already fond of her.[30]

According to family lore, Emily applied to the University of Toronto for admission. However, under the Hincks Act of 1853, the University of Toronto had lost its teaching role and served only as a degree-granting body. Its executive and legislative functions were carried on under the Caput, President and Senate. A candidate for admission applied, not to the university, but to one of the affiliated colleges where courses were given.

The medical faculty of King's College (forerunner of the university) had been closed down, which left two institutions to educate medical students. One was the Toronto School of Medicine on Richmond Street. It was founded, in part, by Dr. John Rolph, who, in 1824 with Dr Charles Duncombe, had started the first and short-lived medical school in St. Thomas. Like Duncombe, Rolph had been a rebel in the 1837 uprising and had fled to the United States. He returned in 1843 and started the Toronto School of Medicine, which soon affiliated with the University of Toronto. By 1863 it was under the direction of Dr. William Thomas Aikins, and Rolph had become the Dean of the Medical Faculty of the University of Victoria College, a degree-granting institution in its own right as well as an affiliate of the University of Toronto. Although Victoria was in Cobourg, its Faculty of Medicine consisted of two medical colleges. One was on Yorkville Avenue, Toronto; the other was *l'Ecole de Médicine et de Chirurgie de Montréal*, opened in 1843 as a medical college for francophones. Because the *école* could grant only diplomas, it affiliated with degree-granting Victoria in 1851, an "unlikely marriage" of "French Canadian Catholics and Protestant evangelicals."[31]

Emily was said to have intended to enter the University of Toronto, but she actually applied to its affiliate, the Toronto School of Medicine. Since an application from a female was unheard of, the Toronto School of Medicine referred Emily's case to the University Senate. She was as unsuccessful with the University of Toronto as she had been with Victoria back in 1853. Again, to her outrage but hardly to her surprise, she was rejected because of her sex.[32] She claimed that she confronted the Vice-President of the University of Toronto, Dr. John McCaul.

He assured her, "The doors of the University are not open to women and I trust they never will be."

Emily retorted, "Then I will make it the business of my life to see that they will be opened, that women may have the same opportunities as men."

In another version of the encounter, McCaul informed her that the decision had been made by the Senate of the University. Emily was said to have replied, "Your Senate may refuse to admit women now, but the day will come when these doors will swing wide open to every female who chooses to apply."[33]

With the rejection of her application by the University of Toronto the iron entered Emily's soul. If she could not train in Canada, she would look south of the border, where there were medical colleges specifically for women.

The date of Emily's application to the University of Toronto is uncertain. At the earliest, 1865 is probably the year she started her medical studies. At that time the course could be as short as two years, or even less.[34] If she had begun in 1863, as has been suggested, she would not have had time to settle John in proper care, nor would she have taught at the Nelles Academy long enough to earn the funds for her studies.

FOUR

Medical Student

ONCE RESOLVED TO STUDY medicine in the United States, Emily had to decide where she would go. Although American women were in the throes of a struggle to establish their right to a medical education, they were years ahead of their Canadian sisters. Emily had the choice of three medical colleges that catered solely to women.

The oldest was the Women's Medical College of Pennsylvania in Philadelphia. It had opened in 1850 with support from the Quakers. The second was the New England Female Medical College in Boston, founded in 1856. The New York Medical College for Women, opened in 1863, was the third; in 1866 it became known as the New York Medical College and Hospital for Women, Homeopathic.[1] Emily elected to enrol in the last, probably because even before 1866, it leaned towards homeopathy to which she was already converted. The Quaker-founded school in Philadelphia would otherwise have been her logical choice. The Philadelphia school and the one in Boston each taught traditional medicine — sometimes called "allopathic." Physicians of orthodox medicine referred scornfully to homeopathics and eclectics as "sectarians."

The New York Medical College for Women had been founded in New York City by Dr. Clemence Sophia Lozier, who had graduated from the Syracuse Medical College in 1853. In 1860, Lozier began teaching classes to women in her own home in New York City — the nucleus of her college and hospital.[2] If Emily was not already a suffragist when she left Mount Pleasant, her experience under Lozier soon made her one. Lozier was a close friend of such well-known suffragists as Elizabeth Cady Stanton and Susan Brownwell Anthony, and she introduced Emily to both women.[3] Mrs. Stanton had been the first recording secretary of the board of trustees of Lozier's school. Miss Anthony, also of a Quaker family, would one day lecture in Canada at Dr. Stowe's request.[4]

When Emily Stowe began her studies, the field of medicine was a mixture of recent discoveries, hidebound conservatism, and some quackery. Scientists were beginning to understand some of the causes and natural history of diseases. In 1798, Edward Jenner of Gloucester, England, had proved that smallpox could be prevented by inoculation with a vaccine made from cowpox. The discovery should have been universally welcomed. But, even 100 years later Dr. Alfred Russell Wallace wrote "Vaccination a Delusion — the Penal Enforcement and Crime." Wallace claimed that the black death disappeared because of improved sanitation, and smallpox had been reduced for the same reason. (He also defended phrenology and hypnotism as legitimate branches of medicine.)[5]

The stethoscope, to help in diagnosis of conditions of the heart and lungs, had been devised by Leopold Auenbrugger in Vienna in 1761, and improved by René Laennec in 1816. Louis Pasteur (1822-1895) in France, evolving his theory of diseases, concluded that some were spread by micro-organisms. Applying the discoveries of Pasteur to surgical practice, the English surgeon, Joseph Lister, introduced the use of carbolic acid to kill bacteria in the operating room, and thus opened the era of aseptic surgery.

Anaesthetics were making possible more complex surgical procedures. In 1800 Humphrey Davy published his researches into the use of nitrous oxide (laughing gas) and suggested its use in surgery. Michael Faraday, one of Davy's assistants, suggested ether, which was easier to produce. Chloroform, first prepared in 1831 in Europe, was used in oral medicines, but in 1847, Sir James Simpson (1811-1870) the Scottish surgeon, replaced ether with chloroform as an inhalation anaesthetic because it caused less nausea and vomiting.[6]

Hand in hand with genuine advances in medical knowledge and hygiene went quackery and other doubtful practices. The advertising pages of newspapers were filled with bewitching appeals to buy better health through magnetic fluids, galvanic belts, electric insoles and electromagnetic wristbands.[7] Patent medicines and nostrums, then as now, satisfied the public demand for a panacea. At a time when the temperance movement was gathering momentum, signatories to the pledge, all unwitting, were drinking large amounts of alcohol in the medicines they consumed.[8]

Politically, too, 1865 was an interesting time for a Canadian in New York City. The bloody civil war between two giants, the Union and the Confederacy, ended with the surrender of General Robert E. Lee to General Ulysses S. Grant at Appomattox Courthouse on the ninth of April, by which time Emily had probably started her studies under Dr. Lozier. Then, on the night of the fourteenth, President Abraham Lincoln was assassinated at Ford's Theatre in Washington. Already the Attorney General of Canada, John A. Macdonald, had spies keeping an eye on the Irish of the Fenian Brotherhood, who were threatening to invade Canada as soon as the Irish of the Union Army were demobilized. They plotted to use these campaign veterans to establish in Canada an Irish republic in exile, far from Britain's shores where, they assumed, transporting a large army would be more difficult than to the island so close to home base. Macdonald also thought he could use the Fenian menace to promote a confederation of all the British North American provinces, partly for mutual defence. On some of her journeys home by train, Emily may well have had as her travelling companions members of the Brotherhood sent to spy in Canada.

New York was overwhelming for a woman whose notion of a big city was provincial Toronto. The population in 1865 was about 1,300,000, crowded on Manhattan and in burgeoning suburbs on Long and Staten islands.[9] New York was the main port of entry for thousands of immigrants, many of whom subsisted in filthy tenements with inadequate sanitation. Some would make their way to other parts of the nation, but all too many were stranded with no money to move on, reduced to begging, or to working for starvation wages if they could find jobs.

In New York the women's suffrage movement was well under way. It had been enhanced by the work women had done during the civil war, while earlier, in 1859, the first Women's Rights Convention had taken place in the city.[10] Emily was quick to perceive that women's suffrage and the advancement of women in the field of medicine were inseparable goals. After she had qualified and was back home, she would have much to say to President John McCaul and others of his stripe!

Not only in the slum tenements were the sanitary facilities inadequate. In 1857, two thirds of the registered deaths were of children under the age of five. Epidemics of typhoid, typhus and cholera, so prevalent in the slums where poor immigrants were forced to dwell, spread to the population as a whole. There were doctors enough, but their training was poor. A few had attended a medical college for one or two years, but many had merely apprenticed with older physicians.[11] Dr. Lozier's hospital was established while Emily was in New York, to give students clinical experience, and to benefit poor women and children. The rich could be cared for in their homes. Hospitals, other than military ones, were mainly to provide care to the poor in sanitary conditions not available to them elsewhere. Before the opening of the hospital, the *New York Times* published a series of articles on the merits and necessity of female medical education. The newspaper discussed the need for the New York Medical College for Women to establish its own hospital. Before it finally opened, women from Dr. Lozier's school were allowed into Bellevue Hospital for their clinical experience.[12]

As at the Provincial Normal School, Emily learned quickly and excelled at her examinations and practical work. Until 1865, almost certainly the year Emily arrived, Dr. Lozier's curriculum had been conventional. In fact, the school had been a traditional one when it was founded in 1863; Lozier did not adopt homeopathic practices in the beginning. Not until the 1865-6 session, did the school announce that the law of "simila" would be recognized. At the same time it stressed that homeopathic teachings had only been *added* to all the branches of medical science.[13] When Emily entered the medical college, the curriculum embraced pathology, principles and practice of medicine, anatomy, physiology, hygiene, obstetrics, medical jurisprudence, clinical and operative surgery, materia medica (pharmacology and pharmacy), diseases of the chest, chemistry and toxicology. By the school's third session, when Emily probably entered the school, Dr. Lozier had added professors from the New York Homeopathic Medical College to her faculty. The staff of some nine professors included both men and women; Lozier's own son, Dr. Abraham W. Lozier, was the professor of chemistry and toxicology.[14] Most were part-time, taught elsewhere and had their own practices.

When Emily arrived in New York City there was a hospital for women and children run by a woman practitioner who regarded Dr. Lozier and her homeopathic leanings with contempt. Elizabeth Blackwell had entered the medical college at Geneva, New York, in 1847 through a fluke. Blackwell had attended medical lectures in Cincinnati, but she wanted to study at an eastern medical college, and if none would accept her she had resolved to go to Europe. Upon receiving Blackwell's application, the dean of the Geneva school asked his male students whether they would tolerate her presence. As much for the novelty of the situation as from altruism, the students voted "Aye," and Elizabeth was in. She graduated in 1849, having attended for two full terms. Immediately afterwards the Geneva Medical College barred the entry of all women students.[15] Blackwell studied for two more years in Europe before she settled in New York, where, in 1854, she opened a dispensary. In 1857 it became the New York Infirmary for Women and Children, a general hospital where women doctors who had trained in Philadelphia and Boston could gain clinical experience.[16] While she was studying abroad, Dr. Blackwell had become a friend of Florence Nightingale. Like Miss Nightingale, she believed that nurses were needed at the front to care for sick and wounded soldiers, so that when the civil war broke out she established the Ladies Relief Committee. Snubbed by the Army Medical Department, she did not hesitate to appeal directly to President Lincoln. The Sanitary Commission, set up in June, 1861, was the outcome. Throughout the war some 2,000 women went to the front as nurses, of whom Dr. Blackwell trained about 100.[17]

Blackwell was conservative and believed in traditional medicine.

In 1868, after Emily had qualified and had left New York City, Blackwell opened her own Women's Medical College of the New York Infirmary in response to the faculty changes at Lozier's school, of which she disapproved.[18] She set very high standards — a three-year course, graded curriculum, and a board of examiners that included some of the most capable male physicians in New York.[19] Many medical schools were allowed to qualify doctors in under three years. Emily was one of these, but, as at the Provincial Normal School, her high intelligence and zeal made up for any deficiencies in her training.

In fact, the medical training Emily received at the New York Medical College for Women, Homeopathic, was thorough by the standard of the time, and she had no need to apologize or feel inferior to any other practitioner. Graduates of the Lozier school, for practical reasons, made some use of drugs or surgical procedures. While male physicians were often accused of prescribing drugs and performing operations too readily, surviving records for the New England Female Medical College, the Massachusetts General and Boston Lying-in Hospitals show that the frequency in the use of drugs and invasive procedures were the same regardless of the sex of the doctor.[20]

Although the exact date of her entry into the New York Medical College and Hospital for Women, Homeopathic, is in some doubt, the date of Emily's graduation was 1867 — the year that four provinces entered into a Canadian confederation, in part prompted by the Fenian menace.[21]

In 1866, while Emily was still studying in New York, the Fenian Brotherhood staged three raids into the Canadas. The most serious came from across the Niagara River, culminating in the Battle of Ridgeway on the second of June. Emily's journey by train, to and from New York City, took her either through Buffalo or Ogdensburg, both border towns with railway terminals where Fenians were gathering. The braggart and exaggerated reports in the New York newspapers on Fenian plans were alarming to one whose family was in Canada West. Emily had no knowledge of how disorganized and ineffective the Fenians were, nor how wide the gap was between bravado and performance. The Attorney General of Canada West, John A. Macdonald, through spies who fraternized in bars with loose-tongued members of the Brotherhood, was well informed on Fenian aspirations. For the most part his militia responded promptly to news of danger.

The fourth annual commencement of the New York Medical College for Women was an impressive occasion. It took place at Steinway Hall, on 14th Street, and was well attended, especially by ladies. The choir of Dr. Osgood's church sang the opening anthem, and the diplomas were conferred by the Reverend Dr. Burchard. Mrs. Emily H. Stowe was one of nine graduates whose names were listed in a newspaper report.[22] Soon afterwards Emily packed her belongings for her return home.

By the early summer of 1867 when, according to their politics, Canadians were either celebrating or mourning the confederation of the first of July, Emily was at home as Dr. Stowe, but not yet ready to set up her practice. She had decided to spend a few months gaining practical experience under Dr. Joseph Lancaster, the old acquaintance from Norwich who was then practising in London.[23] (His house, like the Stowe houses in Mount Pleasant, was also octagonal in shape.)

Meanwhile, Aunt Cordelia remained in charge of the three Stowe children, Augusta, now ten, John Howard, six, and Frank, four. Their father, John, was still convalescent from tuberculosis. Emily's parents remained in Norwichville. Of her sisters, Paulina had married John Duncan and Ethelinda had chosen Martin John McLellan. The two youngest, Hannah and Ella, were each contemplating following in Emily's footsteps, by going to New York for medical training.

In 1867, the year of Emily's return home, a physician had to satisfy one of three separate medical boards — for physicians and surgeons, for eclectics, or for homeopathics.[24] In choosing a form of internship with Dr. Lancaster, Emily had two motives. The first was that Lancaster, too, was of Quaker stock and would treat her as an equal;[25] the second, that as a graduate of a homeopathic school, she could expect to receive registration more readily from the Homeopathic Board in Ontario than from the members of the physicians' and surgeons' board. Emily regarded Lancaster as a capable practitioner who had knowledge of how diseases spread. In 1866, when cholera threatened London, he wrote the Board of Health that he believed the disease was caused by infinitesimal fungi, and that disinfectants would control it.

Despite orthodox physicians' disapproval of a homeopath, the board acted on Lancaster's advice, and the epidemic did not materialize.[26] Towards the end of the year, Emily left London for Toronto and advertised in the *Globe* that she had established a practice in the city.[27] In the *Toronto Directory* for 1868-9 she was listed as Stowe, Emily H. M.D., Alma Terrace House, 39 Richmond East.[28]

When she attempted to obtain a licence to practise, she found herself caught in the midst of changes in the licensing regulations. A Medical Act to regulate practitioners' qualifications had been passed in 1865. Now a new Ontario Medical Act was before the Ontario Legislature to consolidate earlier Acts and to implement the Act of 1865. The old medical boards were to be amalgamated into one Medical Council of the recently constituted College of Physicians and Surgeons of Ontario, on which representatives of physicians and surgeons, homeopaths and eclectics would sit. The secretary of the Homeopathic Medical Board was to submit five names — those who received the most votes from the eligible practitioners — to the Registrar of the Council of the College of Physicians and Surgeons of Ontario, as homeopathic members for the next three years. For purposes of membership, homeopaths and eclectics were treated equally.[29] The Act passed in 1869, but the three categories of practitioners were still listed in the *Medical Directory* under Physicians and Surgeons, Homeopaths, and Eclectics. Qualifications for licences under the new Medical Council included licentiates of the former Homeopathic Medical Board of Upper Canada, but Emily's application for a licence as a homeopath was too late for acceptance by the College of Physicians and Surgeons of Ontario under the new consolidated rules.

Under Section 15 of the 1869 Act, all graduates of medical colleges in the United States had to matriculate and attend one full course of lectures at a school recognized by the Medical Council of the College of Physicians and Surgeons of Ontario.[30] This item was not unreasonable as it applied to men, and it was a sensible safeguard to ensure that only qualified practitioners would work in Ontario. For Emily the measure was a disaster, since none of the Canadian medical schools recognized by the Council would accept a woman candidate.

She saw no alternative but to set up practice without a licence.

Hannah Howard Jennings, 1809-1888, mother of Dr. Emily Stowe. Drawing in chalk. (Courtesy Norwich and District Archives.)

Mary Ann Southwick Treffrey, 1816-1908, in Quaker dress. She was a half-sister of Emily Stowe's mother, Hannah Howard Jennings. (Courtesy Norwich and District Archives.)

The octagonal house in Mount Pleasant, near Brantford, where John and Emily Stowe began their married life in 1856. The house is now a restaurant. (Courtesy author.)

House on Albert Street in Norwich which incorporates the Jennings home. The original house, clapboard and one and a half storeys, has been completely covered by the present structure. (Courtesy author.)

Family group at the cottage on Stowe Island, Muskoka, ca. 1888. Left to right, Belle St. Croix Stowe (Howard's first wife), Howard Stowe, their daughter Emily Howard, Dr. John Gullen (Augusta's husband), Allie St. Croix (Belle's sister), Frank Stowe. (Courtesy Hudson Stowe.)

Frank Jennings Stowe, D.D.S., 1863-1939. Emily's younger son. (Courtesy Hudson Stowe.)

Ann Augusta Stowe Gullen, M.D., 1857–1943, at the time of her graduation from the University of Victoria College, 1883. (Courtesy Victoria University.)

John Howard Stowe, 1861–1926, Emily's elder son, photographed in Muskoka. (Courtesy Diane Stowe Merson.)

Like Great-uncle Solomon, she would overlook the law if it was unfair, confident that in time it would be changed. Some accounts say that she simply paid a fine regularly. In fact, at that time many men practised without a licence, and there were very few prosecutions. Even those who were fined frequently ignored the magistrates and never paid.[31]

Emily chose Toronto because of its size. The larger the centre the better the chance of finding patients who would accept her as a doctor. Her assumption was correct, for scarcely a year after she set up practice she had to move to larger premises in a house at 135 Church Street. She let it be known that her specialty was the diseases of women and children, and she styled herself as Dr. Emily H. Stowe, M.D., in defiance of the regulations.[32] By that time John Stowe may have recovered sufficiently to join his family, although his name does not show up in the *Toronto Directory* until 1873.

Since she had no licence, Emily did not try to obtain hospital privileges, which in any case she did not need. Whatever her concern for the fate of the poor, the main recipients of hospital care, she had to earn money to support herself and the children, to cover John's treatment, and, probably, to pay back her family for loans made while she was away in New York. Since those who could afford to pay usually expected to be cared for in their own homes, Emily's practice consisted of house calls, with the dispensary at 135 Church Street. The main hospital was the Toronto General, started as the York General in 1822, which had continued with various interruptions and changes in locations. Emily had more sense than to become embroiled in the affairs of the Toronto General, where staff and students of the medical schools were at war amongst themselves. The Toronto School of Medicine and the Victoria College Medical Faculty had long been fighting over the use of the hospital facilities.[33]

Meanwhile, she made her rounds and prepared, in her own dispensary, the few medicines she prescribed. Her reputation among the women of Toronto soared. For women and their children the arrival of Dr. Stowe in their midst seemed like a breath of fresh air. This confident, warm, common-sense practitioner could not help but engender a large following.

Male physicians who specialized in women's diseases were

looked down on by their colleagues. Ezra H. Stafford observed as late as the turn of the twentieth century:

> More perhaps in the past than in the present there has been felt a certain tacit contempt for the "woman's physician," whose popularity in that quarter is generally due to qualities extraneous to the scientific practice of his profession.[34]

Stafford went on to claim that these doctors were often summoned for no better reason than to amuse women who had not enough to do. In some quarters the very name "female physician" stood for abortionist. Emily Stowe's battle for equality, as a doctor and as a person, was only beginning, and she had far to go.[35]

FIVE

Dr. Stowe
versus Dr. Trout

THE *TORONTO DIRECTORY* FOR 1870 sheds light on an important undercurrent in the story of Dr. Emily Stowe. Edward Trout was also listed as living at 135 Church Street. He was editor and, with his brother John, founder of a periodical, the *Monetary Times*. Emily was renting part of her house to Edward and his wife, Jenny. Mrs. Trout was ten years younger than their landlady and was very much Emily's disciple. The two women came from similar backgrounds. Like Emily, Jenny had grown up on a farm, north of Stratford; also like Emily, Jenny had been a teacher. Both women were ardent in their desire to foster women's rights, and Emily soon had Jenny converted and willing to study medicine. The two made frequent applications to the Toronto School of Medicine. Finally, in 1870, the president of the school, Dr. William Thomas Aikins, agreed to let them attend classes during the 1870-1871 session. For Emily, this meant that she could qualify to take the examination set by the Medical Council.[1] What Jenny Trout's plans were after the session was not obvious at the time. She may have gone along to keep Emily company, since the one session would not have taken her far towards a medical qualification.

The months spent attending lectures were among the most uncomfortable in the lives of both women. The male medical students bitterly resented the presence of the two females who were invading their territory. They felt threatened by the brazen women who refused to fit into their conventional place in society. Their behaviour was not unusual, for much the same display of bad manners went on in classes in American medical schools when they became coeducational. One of Jenny Trout's friends recalled that while the two women were attending the Toronto School of Medicine, "playful activities of some members of the school were in the way of obnoxious sketches on the wall. There were so many artists, or at least sketches, that the walls of a classroom had to be whitewashed four times during the session."

While male students delighted in leaving objects intended to shock on chairs, the professors were no better. They were not above telling dirty stories; the tactics of all the men were directed at forcing the women to withdraw. Jenny, who was shy and retiring, might have done so, but not Emily. Finally, one of the two, most likely Emily for Jenny would surely have lacked the courage, told a lecturer that if he did not clean up his language she would tell his wife. That worked wonders; afterwards the heckling became subdued and was easier to tolerate.[2]

With the ending of the miserable session, Emily had moved a step closer to being licensed in that she had put in her time at a recognized medical school. She had still to present herself before the Medical Council of the College of Physicians and Surgeons of Ontario but, after some deliberation, she declined to subject herself to the members' scrutiny. Since she had rocked the sedate boat of the profession, she suspected the board would not pass her. She had another reason for believing she would not be acceptable. Although there would be homeopaths on the Council, the representatives of physicians and surgeons outnumbered them and might overrule them. These were reasons enough for not going before the Council, but she had yet another objection. She was so angry over the way she had been treated that she decided to remain without a licence until the Council was prepared to beg her to accept one.

Jenny Trout, too, had had enough, for the time being, of the Toronto medical establishment; but the one session had whetted her appetite. She was determined to go to the United States, as Emily had done, for medical training. Emily encouraged her and eventually Jenny decided to enter the Women's Medical College of Pennsylvania in Philadelphia, rather than the New York Medical College and Hospital for Women, Homeopathic, a choice that may not have pleased Dr. Stowe. Jenny had another friend, Amelia Tefft, who resolved to become a doctor too, and in 1872 the two ladies left together for Philadelphia.[3] With the departure of Jenny and Amelia, a rift began to open between the Trouts and the Stowes; while Jenny was away, her husband moved out of the Stowe house and set up residence at 228 Sherbourne Street.

The *Toronto Directory* for 1873 reveals that John Stowe had been reunited with his wife and children; he is shown as a bookkeeper living at 135 Church Street. Emily and John soon decided that he needed a new occupation. Although John had recovered from tuberculosis, he was not strong enough to resume his trade as a builder and carriage-maker, and he was too talented to be satisfied with bookkeeping. With Emily's backing, he decided to become a dentist. At the time there was no school of dentistry in any part of Canada. A privately operated Canada College of Dentistry had been opened in 1869 but it closed after about a year. The Royal College of Dental Surgeons, the licensing body established by an Act of Parliament in 1868, attempted to found a dental school in 1870, but it had closed after one session.[4]

In 1873, the only way for John Stowe to qualify was through apprenticeship, indentured to a licensed dentist for two years. In November, 1875, the Royal College of Dental Surgeons of Ontario opened the first viable dental school. One of the professors was James Branston Willmott. During the preceding two years, Willmott had been giving evening lectures to indentured students to prepare them to pass the examination necessary to qualify for a licence from the Royal College of Dental Surgeons of Ontario.[5] John may have been among the students who attended these lectures. He passed the examination and received his licence in 1875. This was about the same time as the Royal College of Dental Surgeons, as the new school was named, was opened.[6]

When John began to practise dentistry the house became so overcrowded that the Stowes moved to 111 Church Street. Emily, still practising without a licence, could feel that the family was at last on its feet, although John would never be as robust as she. She was cheerfully ignoring the medical establishment, when Jenny Trout and Amelia Tefft returned to Toronto in 1875. Both women had successfully completed their training after three years at the Women's Medical College of Pennsylvania. Amelia, who had no plans to set up in practice, did not intend to apply for a licence, but Jenny, to Emily's dismay, announced that she was going to be examined by the Medical Council.

Since Jenny had attended a session of lectures at the Toronto School of Medicine and had qualified in the United States at a traditional school, she felt confident that she would pass the examination. Besides, Jenny's quiet manner might not ruffle the feathers of the Council members as Emily's more bristling style would be certain to do. Jenny passed easily and was registered on the thirteenth of May, 1875.[7] This was the end of their friendship, and the beginning of rivalry and enduring bitterness. Emily Stowe was the first woman doctor to practise in Ontario, but Jenny Trout was the first to be licensed.

Before the year ended, Solomon Jennings sold the house in Norwichville and at age seventy-three he retired as bailiff. Afterwards Solomon and Hannah lived in various places, most likely with their daughters, Paulina and Ethelinda, both of whom resided in the vicinity of Norwich.

Meanwhile, Hannah and Ella, Emily's two youngest sisters, had become qualified doctors in New York, but they decided not to tackle the Ontario medical establishment. As well, in 1868, Hannah had become the wife of an American, Charles Kimball, and they resided in New York. Hannah never practised medicine, but Ella, who remained single, was a successful practitioner in New York City. Her business card stated that she was "Medical Director of the Health Specialty Co., 28 West 3rd St. Diseases of Women and Children a Specialty; office hours 11 a.m. to 5 p.m."[8] Both women were as interested as Emily in women's rights and sought to foster them.[9] All three Jennings sisters who had become doctors avidly followed the efforts of American suffragists to obtain the vote.

In May, 1869, Susan Anthony and Elizabeth Cady Stanton organized the National Woman Suffrage Association to fight for the right of women to vote in federal elections. The same year, suffragist Lucy

Stone and a Presbyterian minister in Brooklyn, New York, Henry Ward Beecher, founded the American Woman Suffrage Association, which favoured gradual enfranchisement of women, state by state. (Henry Ward Beecher was a brother of the abolitionist Harriet Beecher Stowe — no relation to Emily's husband — who wrote *Uncle Tom's Cabin*.) In 1870, the United States Congress passed the Fifteenth Amendment to the constitution, granting the franchise to male ex-slaves. Susan Anthony interpreted the amendment as enfranchising American women. In Rochester, New York, two years later, Susan and twelve other suffragists registered and voted. All thirteen, with three inspectors, were arrested. Only Susan was brought to trial. She was fined $100 which she refused to pay, and the judge dismissed her rather than stir up emotions by putting her in jail. Emily, Hannah and Ella saw conviction without punishment as a very small step forward.

Another of the sisters, Cornelia, who had been the mother-substitute to the Stowe children while Emily was in New York, had meanwhile carved out her own career. Her first husband had died, and she moved to Detroit where she opened an antique business. As she prospered, she added a small art gallery to display the works she was able to afford. Other dealers were intrigued by this woman, so knowledgeable about beautiful works of art, but who still retained the plain dress of a Quaker.[10] Along the way she met and married a Cleveland lawyer, a future Judge of the County of Cuyahoga Common Pleas, named Daniel H. Tilden. In 1874, the Tildens made a visit to England, where Cornelia inspected the home of Thomas Carlyle in Chelsea. When the couple returned to Cleveland, Cornelia, with the Jennings sisters' penchant for giving lectures, delivered a report on the Carlyle home before the Ladies' Club. Like her medical sisters, Cornelia was happy on her feet addressing an audience.[11]

Now that John was better, Emily began taking a much more active part in the women's rights movement, initially by attending a meeting of the American Society for the Advancement of Women in Cleveland, Ohio. As usual, the American women were well ahead of their Canadian counterparts. Emily returned to Toronto convinced that the time had come for a similar organization in Canada. The result, in November, 1876, was the Toronto Women's Literary Social and Science

Club (the name was usually shortened to the Women's Literary Club.) It met each Thursday at one of the members' homes to discuss ways to improve their status. The women chose the name for their club deliberately, to disarm the general public who would have regarded a more revealing title as subversive. The articulated aim of the Literary Club was to "secure a free interchange of thought and feeling upon every subject that pertains to woman's higher education, including her moral and physical welfare."[12] Among the first members were Miss Helen Archibald, Mrs. Donald McEwan, Mrs. Anna Parker, Miss Jenny Gray, and Mrs. Sarah Ann Curzon, who was a strong advocate of temperance in the use of alcohol. By temperance most members meant, not moderation, but prohibition.

At each meeting one of the members gave a paper. One, by Miss Archibald, was entitled "The Enfranchisement of Women." In it she refuted such nonsense that participation in politics would cause women to lose their femininity and become coarse and vulgar. Emily spoke on the need for better education for girls. Other topics were temperance and all aspects of hygiene. One result of their efforts was that factories and stores opened separate toilets for women employees.

Emily gloried in doing research on a wide variety of topics, such as monetary policy, and the causes of crime. By this time in her life, she had ceased to think of herself as a Quaker and no longer dressed like one. Henry J. Morgan, who wrote a series of books which he called *Canadian Men and Women of the Time,* described Dr. Stowe as having "outgrown all religious creeds" and become a truth-seeker. She called herself "a mental scientist", and "a scientific socialist."[13] While Emily was becoming a free thinker, John and the children, more conventional, attended the Metropolitan Methodist Church. Emily's Quaker background showed through in the bulldog tenacity with which she pursued her objective of equality.

While Emily fought her battle, the leading male medical practitioners in Toronto who wanted health reform were engaged in a conflict with which she was in sympathy. They were sparring with the City Council over the issue of the "sanitary idea." Some doctors were taking the stand, which originated in Britain, that the state should be responsible for preventing outbreaks of infectious diseases. As the city grew larger, there was more danger from garbage left in back lanes, from poorly maintained privies and cesspools, and from contaminated wells.[14] Since 1834, when the city was incorporated and empowered to establish a Board of Health, the city fathers had done so only when an epidemic such as cholera, typhus, scarlet fever or diphtheria threatened. But once the danger had past, the board was dissolved.

Advocates of the "sanitary idea" wanted a Board of Health retained on a permanent basis to keep the city clear of refuse, and to stop the dumping of slaughterhouse remains, sewage and other disgusting substances into Ashbridge's Bay and Toronto Harbour. At the heart of the matter lay patronage. The Tory-dominated Council wanted to control the Board of Health; by creating a permanent board, the members had an opportunity to use appointments as rewards. Also, Council was reluctant to commit funds when an emergency had passed.[15] Emily was aware that these public health measures were desirable. Apart from smallpox, many diseases were spread to all classes through dirty conditions amongst the poor. While they left most of the talking to the men, the members of the Women's Literary Club were every bit as concerned with preventive medicine and the importance of a healthy environment. In time, Emily was convinced, women could hasten such improvements, but only if they had the power to influence the civic politicians. Until that time, they were better off working to achieve the right to vote, and their first objective ought to be enfranchisement for municipal elections. Then people could speak not only of city fathers, but also for city mothers.

While Emily's busy medical practice continued, Dr. Jenny Trout was becoming more and more a thorn in her side. The quiet little upstart was threatening to overtake Dr. Stowe, with the help of her husband's resources. Where Emily had to depend on herself, Edward Trout was able to finance expensive equipment and facilities. By 1877, the Trouts had opened the grand Therapeutic and Electrical Institute, proprietors Dr. Jenny Trout and her friend, Amelia Tefft. Their premises occupied four lots on Jarvis Street, numbers 272-278.[16] Amelia was not licensed, but could operate under Jenny's wing. Besides, Emily Stowe was living testimony that one could practise nicely without a licence.

The treatment of disease by electricity was all the rage, and Jenny's establishment, which could accommodate sixty patients, featured the latest in up-to-date apparatus. Doctors were making use of both galvanic (direct) and faradic (alternating) current.[17] While Dr. Lancaster was among the first to try electricity on his patients, Emily remained skeptical. But she soon found that she had to offer limited electric treatments, in order to keep abreast of Jenny Trout and their male rivals.[18] Emily resented the unwarranted extravagance; she was able to cover the family's expenses but she was not becoming wealthy from her practice. In 1875, *The Globe* published an article entitled "The Singular Poverty of the Medical Profession," stating that the average income of a doctor was about $1,200 per annum, while a clergyman earned well over $2,000.[19]

One description of the electrical treatment apparatus that has survived is the "Electrikure" — a shiny silver cylinder filled with rocks which was placed on the head to cure a headache. At the same time a crock of water with wet disks was attached to an ankle by elastic bands — but with no current.[20] This was pure quackery, but some treatments relieved muscular pain and at least did no harm. An electric belt, supposed to cure "sexual debility," impotence and atrophy in men, contained a series of batteries. The electric current passed from the belt to a pendulum suspended over the affected area.[21]

Jenny Trout operated a free dispensary for the poor, and took in needy young girls and helped to educate them. She opened branch offices in Hamilton and Brantford, and went about the province giving lectures on medicine. While Emily was president of the Women's Literary Club, Jenny was vice-president of a rival organization, the Association for the Advancement of Women, and president of the Women's Christian Temperance Union (founded in 1874). Emily was losing ground, both as the leading woman physician and as a suffragist. Jenny, childless, had a wealthy husband. Emily was still the major breadwinner with three children to raise. As well, she still ran a large practice, all the while continuing the campaign for women's rights.

In 1877, Augusta turned twenty, while John Junior, generally called Howard, was sixteen and Frank fourteen. Augusta was an enthusiastic supporter of her mother; she became a vocal suffragist herself and assisted in the crusade for the vote. Unlike her mother, she was interested in high fashion, and liked to dress in the very latest style. While she did not particularly like the costume the American suffragist Amelia Bloomer designed, on at least one occasion Augusta dressed in bloomers and rode a bicycle down Yonge Street. She carried out her prank to demonstrate that she, and all other women, had every right to wear any outfits they chose, no matter how outlandish.[22]

The two boys, still at school, were ambivalent over their mother's career, and not certain they liked being part of a household where traditional roles were reversed. In the homes of their friends, Mother stayed at home attending to housekeeping duties, while Father left the house after breakfast, returning for an evening meal or often, in so small a city as Toronto, for a noon dinner. In the Stowe house, Father was usually on hand, in his dental office or resting quietly when fatigue overcame him. Mother was usually on the run, coming in from her rounds and dashing off to her next meeting or lecture as soon as a meal was over, or when her office was empty of patients. Living an unconventional life could be an embarrassment to young people who, then as now, tended to be conservative and wanted to be like their peers. Their father's companionship was available at home, but one way the boys could snatch some time with their mother was by driving the horse for her on her rounds. Frank, in particular, was never happier than when he went on rounds. He remembered that the man who cared for his mother's horse was a Black, and his name was Avery.

Meanwhile, medical education in Toronto had undergone some changes. The university, still bound by the Hincks Act, had no teaching facilities, but it continued to grant medical degrees to candidates from the Toronto School of Medicine, and now from the Trinity Medical College as well. Also, and most important, the university was the body that dispensed the medals and prizes.

There were only two schools of medicine in the city, because Victoria's Medical Faculty had folded owing to lack of funds, staff defections and declining enrollment. Part of the cause was competition from the Toronto School of Medicine and Trinity. In 1874, the medical students of Victoria went in a body to the Toronto School of Medicine.

Victoria still granted its own degrees to medical graduates, but it no longer operated its own medical faculty in Toronto. The Victoria Medical Faculty consisted only of the *école* for Francophones in Montreal.[23]

Trinity Medical Faculty had originated in 1850, when the college absorbed the independent Upper Canada Medical School which had started in 1843.[24] Candidates to Trinity, the Anglican college, had to sign the Thirty-nine Articles, certifying that they were adherents of the Church of England. In 1855, unable to attract sufficient Anglican students, the staff members tried to have the medical school made secular, but they met with bitter opposition from Bishop Strachan. The school closed the following year.[25] The death of Strachan, in 1867, opened the way for a revival, this time without the Anglican restriction, and in March, 1871, the first professors were appointed.[26] By 1877, rivalry between these two schools of medicine was as fierce as it had been between the previous two. This time the issue was prizes and medals. The Toronto School of Medicine wanted to exclude the Trinity students from the University of Toronto examinations, to prevent them competing for the prizes and medals.

As a result, the legislature passed an act to make the Trinity Medical College independent of the University of Trinity College. Thus the school could affiliate with any university it chose. Trinity Medical College selected the University of Toronto, which made the students eligible to share in the medals and prizes.[27] A student registered at Victoria, but attending the Toronto School of Medicine, could now receive a degree from Victoria and share in the prizes, because Victoria did not have its own medical school in Toronto. A student registered at the Trinity Medical College, no longer part of Trinity College, could receive a degree from the University of Toronto and share in the prizes and medals. By that time, a medical degree required four years of study, and a candidate had to be at least twenty-one years of age at graduation. Emily kept a keen eye on these changes, for they held serious implications for her daughter.

Augusta had decided she wanted to study medicine. Before sending her to the United States as a last resort, Emily resolved to enter the ring for one more round with the Canadian university establishment. The only route to success, she had long ago discovered, was through persistence. She remembered the words of Professor John McCaul, the Vice-president of the University of Toronto in 1853, who once told her he hoped the doors of the university would never be open to a woman. They still had not opened, but McCaul, then the President of University College, was getting up in years. He and his kind could not last much longer. In all likelihood, as younger, less hidebound academics replaced them, the doors would finally open. Emily hoped the university would relent in time to serve Augusta.

SIX

Licensed at Last

BY 1877, EMILY THOUGHT she could see light in the distance. A year after Edward Blake was installed as Chancellor in 1876, the University of Toronto Senate made the decision to establish examinations for women.[1] They would be admitted to University College. The storm broke immediately, leading to a controversy that went on for years. Daniel Wilson, due to become President of University College in 1880 on the retirement of Dr. John McCaul, proposed that a separate college should be established for women. This fuelled the argument. Emily Stowe was gratified by the decision, but appalled at the stalling tactics of Professor Wilson and others. No doubt she suspected Professor McCaul was supporting them. At the same time, word reaching Toronto from New Brunswick was so heartening that Emily was tempted momentarily to allow Augusta to go there. Mount Allison University had agreed, in 1875, to allow women to take degrees. Wheels turned slowly, but with persistence women could make them turn! Almost at once Emily changed her mind about Mount Allison. If Augusta wanted to become a doctor, the best training was to be found at the Toronto School of Medicine, which had an excellent staff headed by President Aikins.

Dr. William Thomas Aikins had attended Victoria College in Cobourg and the Toronto School of Medicine before seeking further medical education in the United States. In 1850, he received his doctorate from Jefferson Medical College in Philadelphia. He was progressive, the first surgeon in Canada to employ Lister's methods of antiseptic surgery. Dear to Emily's heart, Aikins had long advocated open air treatment of tuberculosis patients (the first sanatorium on the continent was still some years in the future.)[2] Emily had good reason to be grateful to Dr. Aikins, who had permitted her to take, at a Canadian medical school, the classes that were necessary for the licence she still did not have. While she could not look back on those classes with any emotion but anger, Aikins had at least treated her more fairly than most members of the profession.

By 1878, women were allowed to take the University of Toronto entrance examinations but, if they were successful, they could not attend any lectures since no college would admit them. Hoping somehow to break down the barrier and gain entrance to the Toronto School of Medicine, Augusta Stowe, supported by Emily, sat the matriculation examinations for the university set by the Council of the College of Physicians and Surgeons. She failed mathematics but, undaunted, she resolved to try again after further study at home, possibly with a tutor.[3]

Meanwhile, Emily continued working towards women's rights, and had begun to lecture in Toronto and in other centres, wherever she was invited. With each speaking engagement she developed and improved her themes, some of which she called "Woman's Sphere" and "Women in the Professions." She declared that women were more sympathetic than men where illnesses of women and children were concerned. Why, some male doctors had even admitted their inadequacies! She maintained that every woman "ought to understand the laws governing her own being."[4] As well as stressing the need for better education for girls, she thought their studies should embrace homemaking. The Toronto Women's Literary Club remained as active as ever, and was instrumental in persuading store owners to provide chairs for their clerks, many of whom were poorly paid women. Clerks who worked twelve hours a day six days a week, with only a short break for lunch, should not be expected to stand the whole time.[5]

No evidence survives that Emily actually paid a fine for practising medicine without a licence. In one of the many short newspaper biographies, a reporter claims she was threatened with prosecution, but she used an opinion expressed by Dr. Aikins of the Toronto School of Medicine in her own defence. Aikins "gave evidence" (the article does not say where nor identify the case) that if one prescribed "the sawing of a cord of wood as a remedy for physical illness then that one was practising medicine." Defending herself, Emily recalled assisting Dr. Joseph Lancaster of London in the therapeutic use of electricity — evidence enough that she was qualified to practise medicine as in Dr. Aikins' hypothetical case.[6] Yet she could see that practice outside the medical establishment had certain advantages. After Christian Scientists formed a congregation in Toronto, the healer would consult Emily from time to time when faith alone could not help a sick or injured follower.[7]

Emily joined the Women's Christian Temperance Union, but did not take a very active part in it. She considered alcohol a dangerous poison and favoured abstention, but her arch rival, Dr. Jennie Trout, was a leader in the temperance movement. That was reason enough for Emily to stand back from the temperance advocates and concentrate her efforts on the work of the Toronto Women's Literary Club. At one of the meetings she read a paper on alcoholic drinks in which she condemned an article by a Dr. Carpenter who claimed that spirits were a valuable remedy though not nutritious. In Emily's opinion Dr. Carpenter's view was "absurd;" alcohol was injurious and its use ought to be banned.[8]

She considered ways and means of opening a hospital for women that would provide clinical experience for woman doctors who had qualified elsewhere, but her dream was not to become a reality for many years. As surgical techniques became more sophisticated, she could see the need for hospital care for patients other than the indigent. The young could now be cared for in their own Hospital for Sick Children, which had opened in 1875 in a house at 31 Avenue Road. In all her efforts John supported her. His own strength was limited, but he had encouraged her during his convalescence when she was determined to become a doctor. Successful women pioneers in the field of rights have often been blessed with the money to pursue their social and political ideals. Not infrequently they had the backing from like-minded husbands. Canadian suffragists were usually from the middle classes, women who had financial resources and the leisure to be concerned about social and political issues. Women who had to work six days a week had little energy left over to better the lot of themselves and others.

The establishment of a special hospital for children was a step forward in the Toronto health care scene of the 1870s. Yet many still regarded hospitals as necessary only for the indigent. In Belleville, an important centre for the Grand Trunk Railroad, women pressing for a hospital were vilified. The railway, the newspapers protested, brought too many vagrants and paupers as it was; a hospital would only encourage more of them to encamp in the city.[9]

As the 1870s were drawing to a close, the members of the Toronto Women's Literary Club were concerned about public health in the rapidly growing city. By 1881, the population had reached more than 80,000, but the quality of its services had decreased. City water was piped to homes from Toronto Bay, which received sewage and other noxious wastes. Nevertheless, water from the intake pipe in the bay was cleaner than from some private wells situated close to privies and cesspools.[10] The city politicians were not anxious to commit taxpayers' money to improvements, but the Toronto Women's Literary Club, under the leadership of Dr. Stowe, watched with interest as male members of the medical profession vigorously pressed their case.

City councillors could not make up their minds whether preventive medicine should take precedence over curative, or whether they should be combined under a single medical officer. The *Mail* favoured prevention, which required the services of a full time officer and a permanent local board of health. This displeased the members of Council who foresaw a weakening of their influence, with permanent staff replacing appointments by patronage.[11] Sanitation, and the need for properly inspected meat and clean milk were legitimate concerns for the Toronto Women's Literary Club. Proof that the medical profession was becoming more aware of the need for better sanitation lay in the appointment of Dr. William Oldright, in 1876, as professor of sanitary science at the Toronto School of Medicine. Oldright persuaded the premier, then Oliver Mowat, to appoint a select committee of the legislature to study sanitary deficiencies.[12] The committee soon reported that the province needed a permanent central board of health under a Medical Health Officer, but for the moment Premier Mowat was not ready to act on this recommendation. His foot-dragging did not surprise Emily, for she had cause to know how adroit premiers could be at maintaining the status quo.

The Toronto Women's Literary Club was also beginning to think that standards of nursing in hospitals should be raised. Hospitals were cleaner than they had been, but nurses were still uneducated women. At Toronto General Hospital nurses were paid nine dollars a month with board and lodging. They slept in rooms that opened into their wards, and each carried her own knife, fork and spoon in her pocket. None received any formal training.[13]

Yet foremost in Emily's thinking was women's need for political power — the right to vote fully in all elections, municipal, provincial and federal, instead of merely for school trustees. Until women were thus enfranchised they would remain at the mercy of men and could never initiate reforms in nursing or in access to hospitals. She was not able to make use of any existing hospital because, as an unlicensed practitioner and a female, no hospital would admit her patients. In her speeches she never made reference to darkening the doors of a hospital, but she did talk about her visits to private homes:

> In my profession on rounds I have entered houses that were
> in no sense homes — dirty, untidy, unkempt, and not be-
> cause of vice, but because of ignorance and lack of a system
> by which much labour can be performed with a facility and
> ease unknown to the unskilled.

In one such household the woman admitted that she had worked in a factory from the age of nine until her marriage and had never learned to care for a house.[14]

Meanwhile, nursing education in Britain had taken a giant step forward when Florence Nightingale opened the Nightingale School of Nursing at St. Thomas' Hospital, London, in 1860, with fifteen unpaid probationers. It was financed by funds raised in tribute to Miss Nightingale's work in the Crimean War (1853-1856), and it marked the beginning of professional education in nursing. In 1875, the Committee of Management of the Montreal General Hospital consulted Miss Nightingale and arranged for some nurses trained by her to come to Canada. The scheme failed through jealousies and unfair public criticism, and the nurses returned to England.

Then in 1877, the Toronto General Hospital hired Harriet Goldie as a superintendent for a new nurses' training school. Miss Goldie had nursed during the Franco-Prussian War (1870-1871). However, four years of dissent and slow planning were to pass before any probationers actually started their training.[15] In the interval, the first school of nursing opened in 1879 at St. Catharines, Ontario — a time when Augusta Stowe's head was buzzing over news that she might be able to study at Queen's College in Kingston.

Elizabeth Smith of Winona, Ontario, was another young woman with ambitions to become a doctor. She and Augusta probably met earlier in 1879 when they sat the matriculation examination of the University of Toronto. This time both women passed handsomely and Elizabeth returned to Winona to await further developments. Soon she heard that Queen's College was willing to admit a few women, and that it was also offering summer courses in medicine to them. The Kingston medical school, called the Royal College of Physicians and Surgeons, was affiliated with Queen's. Miss Smith wrote to Augusta Stowe, and in July she sent a notice to the *Globe* that "Ladies wishing to study medicine in Canada will hear of something to their advantage by communication with Box 31, Winona."[16] Augusta Stowe wrote that she would be "glad to hear of anything that will be of advantage to me as a Medical Student." However, Emily thought that since the Queen's course was not to be given until the summer of 1880, Augusta should start her training sooner, preferably at the Toronto School of Medicine.

Emily herself wrote to Elizabeth Smith, explaining her opinion. She did not want Augusta to have to delay another full year before beginning a medical course, and she had strong objections to studying through the summer.

No one can study as well than as in cold weather, you cannot dissect, and by the profession generally they would never be recognized as of equal value with the winter courses. There are never the same hospital advantages in summer as winter.

Her next sentence reveals that she could not always conceal some resentment over her own treatment at the hands of the medical profession. "With regard to the excessive value of a Canadian degree, it is more imaginary than real, and if obtained from separate or summer courses its value would fall."[17]

She had been in touch with Reverend Dr. Samuel Nelles, the brother of Dr. William Nelles under whom she had taught at the academy in Mount Pleasant after John became ill in 1863. Samuel Nelles was now the President of Victoria College, and Emily had no compunction over trading on the long-standing friendship between her family and his. She asked that Augusta be accepted as a student by Victoria, a degree-granting university. Acceptance would allow Augusta to enrol at the Toronto School of Medicine under Dr. Aikins. (Victoria had not had its own medical faculty since 1874, but medical students enrolled in Victoria were eligible to attend the Toronto School of Medicine.) If Dr. Nelles would not oblige, the only alternative would be a school in the United States, possibly Dr. Elizabeth Blackwell's establishment in New York City. Dr. Lozier's homeopathic school was still operating, but the experience of Jenny Trout was not forgotten. Augusta would have a better chance of obtaining a licence if she graduated from a traditional medical school. Then, to the delight and relief of all the Stowes, through Dr. Nelles' influence, Augusta was accepted into Victoria College and could enrol in the Toronto School of Medicine. The university issued a certificate dated May, 1879, stating that Augusta Stowe had passed the matriculation examinations required by the Medical Council of the College of Physicians and Surgeons of Ontario.[18]

She did not have an easy time at first, for she was subjected to the same brand of heckling and harassment her mother had endured. Yet she remained resolute, and set out bravely each day to lectures and "practicals" at the school downtown near the Toronto General Hospital. Often there were tears when she came home, but gradually she gained a measure of acceptance. She was hard to dislike; articulate, clever and quick to learn, she was sociable and with a winning manner that would ultimately carry her far in Toronto society and politics. Like her mother, she was essentially feminine; in spite of political activities that many people regarded as unbecoming, neither woman was ever described as "mannish." On at least one occasion, when some male students attempted a disturbance in class, others came to Augusta's aid by siding with her.[19] One, especially, was soon attracted to her — a student registered at the Trinity Medical College named John Gullen. John came of a Scots family that had settled in and around Megantic, Quebec, where his father, Robert, had been a county court judge. On the death of John's mother, in 1864, the Gullens moved to Oxford County, Ontario,[20] where they came to know some of the Jennings relatives. The Stowe home on Church Street became a home away from home for the young man.

When Augusta Stowe entered the Toronto School of Medicine in 1879, she was twenty-two. Her brother, John Howard, aged eighteen, decided on a career in the business world, and in time he became a manufacturer's agent. Sixteen-year-old Frank, however, was considering an education in some field allied with medicine.[21] He decided to become a dentist, like his father, and he would not have to apprentice with a licensed dental surgeon, for now, in Toronto, there was a school he could attend. In 1875, the Royal College of Dental Surgeons of Ontario had established its own dental school, which was called the Royal College of Dental Surgeons — a name that has caused confusion.[22] The course lasted two years, and Frank graduated in 1882.[23]

About the same time as Frank started his training, Emily received the interesting news that she had at last been granted a licence by the Council of the College of Physicians and Surgeons of Ontario. She was probably not too gratified, since by now she had become accustomed to ignoring rules made by men. There were two kinds of crimes, she maintained: those which transgressed divine law, and those which violated man's laws.[24] Woman was under scant obligation to obey laws devised by males, although all should submit to the laws laid down by God. Emily decided what was divine law, rather than relying on clergymen, a throwback to her Quaker past.

The date of Emily's registration was the sixteenth of July, 1880.[25] The item in the *Medical Register* reads, "In practice prior to 1st January 1850. M.D. New York College for Women 1867." The 1850 date must be an error for 1880. However, the entry does not clear up the mystery of exactly how Emily was licensed. Carlotta Hacker, author of *The Indomitable Lady Doctors*, suspected that Emily did take the examination after she finished classes at the Toronto School of Medicine, but failed it. [26] But that does not explain why the Council finally gave in and licensed her. More likely, Emily had become so well-known and had such a fine reputation as a physician that she had become an embarrassment to the College of Physicians and Surgeons of Ontario. The Council would then have broken down and granted the licence to dispose of a vexing irregularity. One way or another, the deed was done, and after practising illegally for thirteen years, Emily became a respectable member of her profession.

Three months before, in April, 1880, Queen's College in Kingston had started a medical course for women, with three students. They were Miss Elizabeth Smith (Shortt), who had written to Augusta the year before, Mrs. Alice Skimmen McGillivray and Miss Elizabeth Robb (Beatty). In her diary, Miss Smith, the future wife of the distinguished scholar, Adam Shortt, recorded that charges for board were $2.50 per week, and that four notebooks, a box of surgical tools, four knives, a hook, a pair of scissors and two forceps had cost her $3.00. Gray's *Anatomy* was a lofty $6.50.[27]

For Emily, the course for women in Kingston was a great leap forward, but she still thought how much better off Augusta was at the Toronto School of Medicine. The three women at Queen's would not qualify until 1884 while Augusta would be ready to take the examinations of the Medical Council of the Royal College of Physicians and Surgeons a year in advance of them.

Emily was the first Canadian woman to practise medicine in Canada; Augusta would be the first to graduate in medicine from a Canadian university. Mother and daughter would try to forget that they could not dislodge Dr. Jenny Trout as the first woman granted a licence to practise medicine in Canada.

SEVEN

Another Stowe First
(1881–1893)

AS THE YEARS PASSED, Emily kept in touch with her family and friends in Norwich. Although Solomon Jennings had sold his freehold property on Lot 7, Concession 4, in Norwichville, in 1875,[1] he and his wife Hannah probably remained in the neighbourhood. Emily's most treasured ties with Norwich were sundered in 1881 when Solomon died at seventy-nine. He was buried, not in the Friends' cemetery in Norwich, but in Toronto's Mount Pleasant Cemetery, where Emily had purchased six plots and had paid $35.00 for their perpetual care. The funeral service took place in the Stowe house before the burial. Later, Hannah Jennings divided her time amongst the homes of her six daughters, and Emily again plunged into her busy round of house calls and suffrage meetings.

The Toronto Women's Literary Club had a new organ to influence public opinion. When Mrs. Sarah Curzon, long a loyal member of the club, was appointed associate editor of the *Canada Citizen*, she arranged for a regular column in support of woman suffrage. This temperance newspaper was the first in Canada to enlist in the cause.[2] The club members continued to present papers on educational topics and, on occasion, papers wholly intended to amuse. The most vital work during 1881 was the organizing of the first deputation to the Ontario Legislature to discuss the enfranchisement of women.[3]

Premier Mowat's long tenure spanned the years 1872 to 1896.

Emily had to deal with him throughout most of her active years in the battle for the vote. The durable premier's response was one that she would hear over and over again. Mowat was sympathetic to the cause, but lamented that he could not carry the legislature with him. The members, not only of the opposition but within his own Liberal Party, were not yet ready to consider woman suffrage. Preparing men to accept women in so traditionally a male sphere would require time and careful persuasion.

Meanwhile, the City of Toronto continued to grow, and the matter of expanded public health facilities was becoming ever more urgent. Emily was as concerned about the need for improved sanitation and the effect of urban growth on the quality of meat and milk as any male doctor, but she remained single-minded in her dedication foremost to women's rights. Enfranchisement was the only practical goal; once women had political power, all else would follow. City Council was discussing the appointment of a medical health officer, but it was still arguing over whether the objectives of the office should be preventive or only curative. The current mayor, William McMurrich, wanted a medical relief officer, to ensure that chronic cases in the Toronto General Hospital would be treated at public expense, rather than become the sole responsibility of the City. Robert Awde, the inspector of licences, wanted stricter bylaws, and Emerson Coatsworth, the city commissioner, was calling for extended powers.[4]

The Ontario Legislature's general committee was investigating the shortcomings of the public health service throughout the province. The committee soon called for a Central Board of Health similar to that operating in Britain. Premier Mowat stalled until after the Ontario Medical Association, formed in 1880, had held its first annual general meeting in 1881. The Association was then in a position to put pressure on the government. Emily did not try to become a member, since she guessed the men would only reject her application. But she applauded the Association's success, when the legislature passed the first Public Health Act in 1882. It gave the City of Toronto a mandate to supervise municipal preventive efforts. The province had now taken action, but the city fathers continued to debate. They disliked, and were fearful of, outside interference in their affairs.

The federal government had come to the aid of the medical profession long before the province. The government of Sir John A. Macdonald had passed a Census and Vital Statistics Act in 1879, which set aside funds to assist the collection of information. When, in 1881, the results were published, doctors had a better idea of the incidence of diseases and where certain types of illness were likely to be concentrated. The province's Medical Act of 1882 enabled Toronto to appoint a Medical Health Officer, and it also provided for a provincial board of health. Moving faster than the city, the legislature appointed Dr. Peter Byrne secretary of the provincial board. Byrne was soon actively promoting the establishment of a local board for the City of Toronto. He was particularly concerned to see that tuberculosis was brought under control, a measure close to Emily's heart.[5]

By 1882, when he was nineteen, Frank Stowe had completed his studies at the Royal College of Dental Surgeons, and he could now put the initials L.D.S. after his name and commence practice. Times had changed, however, since his father had posted those treasured initials outside his office at 111 Church Street. Frank now wanted his doctorate, and his parents agreed. They gave him the financial assistance to spend a year in Philadelphia, where a good programme was available.[6]

For Emily Stowe, the crowning event of 1882 was not in the medical field, although she saw certain ramifications for it. Women made their first, modest advance towards universal suffrage; the door had opened a crack. The Ontario Legislature passed a bill to allow unmarried women, both widows and spinsters, to vote in municipal elections provided they met the same property qualification as men. This was a small but significant victory. Now, Emily knew, there would be a female vote in favour of the appointment of a medical health officer for the city, for most women favoured the move. At the same time, she thought the discrimination against married women made no sense. As long as they, too, held property they should be allowed to vote. She held to the usual prejudice of the time, that anyone who did not own property should not be enfranchised. Property gave a person a sense of responsibility. The specious argument that to allow both spouses in one household to vote would "destroy domestic harmony" was only to be expected.[7] What nonsense, thought Emily, who had spent most of her married life in a house of domestic harmony, where two careers flourished under one roof.

She had no time to rest, not while the provincial and federal governments were still holding out against the vote for women. Emily continued accepting invitations to speak at meetings in Toronto, Brantford, and in many smaller towns in southern Ontario. Her message was usually along the main theme, that there were jobs women were more suited to fulfil than men, that while each sex had its own sphere, both were equal, and that women deserved the same educational opportunities as men. She was appalled at attempts to keep girls out of the grammar schools (at the same time some school boards were accused of packing the grammar schools with girls just to get the provincial grants). One place where she delivered her lecture on the unfair discrimination was at the town hall in Brantford.[8]

From her home in Toronto, she was still leading the fight to have women admitted to the university. When she could spare the time she was taking a petition from house to house gathering signatures. Now that women had a say in municipal government the door to the University of Toronto must surely yield; the opposition would soon melt away. Emily was unimpressed by Goldwin Smith's article in the *Bystander* newspaper:

> If all the young men and women of the wealthier class between the ages of eighteen and twenty-two were to be thrown together in the same colleges Presidents would indeed have to undertake to a formidable extent, in addition to their present functions, the duties of duenna.[9]

About this time at a conference Emily gave a paper that was reported in a Toronto newspaper. Her subject was "Crime, Its Causes and Cures." After again defining the two kinds of crimes as against the laws of man and against divine law, she worked her way towards the message she wanted to get across. The evil force in the world was the concentration of wealth in the hands of the few. In the United States, she informed her audience, 4,147 individuals owned two thirds of the country thereby controlling forty billion dollars. The same trend was evident in Canada, which had its own share of "Shylocks." In the natural world, laws were divine and all forms of life were in harmony, each with its proper sphere. The suppressed position of women was a major cause of crime, and the source was unequal and unjust legislation "and the universal adoption as a rule of business action." The cure would be wise, just legislation. She saw a relationship between tariffs and the increase in crime. If men would study natural sciences, God would help them. In another account of the same speech, the reporter told the readers that Dr. Stowe gave electrical treatment and employed a female masseur.[10]

In 1882, the rivalry between Emily Stowe and Jenny Trout came temporarily to an end. Dr. Trout's Therapeutic and Electrical Institute was not a financial success. She had spread herself too thin, and the heavy pressure of both the practice and the institute proved too much for her health. She had also found the publicity given to her lectures on medicine and to her unique institute taxing. She had run a free dispensary for the poor which she could not afford to retain, and she had seen as many as fourteen patients a day. In addition she had branch offices in Hamilton and Brantford. So Jenny, retired, was no longer competing with Emily in the medical field. As the year drew to a close, Drs. Stowe and Trout were enjoying a brief respite as they worked towards a common objective.

They were part of a group seeking ways and means to open a medical college for women.[11] Closely associated with them was Dr. Michael Barrett, a professor of physiology at the Toronto School of Medicine. Barrett's interest in fostering medical education for women may have arisen from a varied background wherein he had encountered women engaged in many pursuits. Born in England in 1816, he was seventeen when he came with his family to Canada in 1833. At first he earned his living as a sailor out of Penetanguishene. Later he taught school at Newmarket (where he was on the government side during the Rebellion of 1837.) When his father moved to Natchez, Mississippi, Michael joined him, but returned to Canada West in 1843. For two years he studied law in Toronto, then he joined the staff of Upper Canada College as an English master. He entered King's College in 1846, earned B.A. and M.A. degrees, studied medicine, and was licensed to practise in 1852. In addition to teaching at the Toronto

School of Medicine, simultaneously, he was teaching chemistry and physiology at Upper Canada College.[12]

Young Augusta Stowe was also associated with the committee working towards a medical college for women. She was by now in her third year at the Toronto School of Medicine. With her classmates she alternated between class sessions and practical instruction, and clinical experience at the Toronto General Hospital. Because she was accepted as a medical student, few challenged her right to examine patients, although she must have grown accustomed to some disapproving looks wherever she went. As 1882 was ending, she became engaged to John Benjamin Gullen. They were attending different medical schools in Toronto, but were working together on the hospital floors.

By March, 1883, the members of the Toronto Women's Literary Club decided the time had come to show their true colours. The Club must change its name to one that was more relevant. From now on it would have one objective, and the papers delivered would be on that theme. On the ninth, in the City of Toronto Council Chamber, the members of the old literary club held their first meeting as the Toronto Women's Suffrage Association. The behaviour of the city fathers was in contrast to that of the provincial legislators; council was co-operative, whereas the legislators treated women with derision and contempt. At the same time, the city fathers had no power to grant suffrage; lacking any valid responsibility they could support the women without making any real commitment. The good will of the city fathers was cheap. At their inaugural meeting in the council chamber the women passed the resolution, "That in the opinion of this meeting the municipal and parliamentary Franchise should be extended to women who possess the same qualifications which entitle men to vote."

Membership in the new association was open to males as well as females, and the first executive included five men. The president was Mrs. Donald McEwan; the secretary Jenny Foulds, and among the vice presidents were Captain W.F. McMaster, ex-alderman John Hallam, Mrs. S.A. Curzon and Dr. E.H. Stowe.[13]

The Toronto Women's Literary Club had served its purpose. Now, Emily felt, the public knew what the women's aims were. By

1883, most people could accept an association with a name that spelled out its objectives, something they would have thought wanton in 1876.

Frank Stowe soon returned from Philadelphia to put D.D.S. on the sign at 111 Church Street, where he joined his father in the dental office. Emily was becoming more worried about John, who seemed less strong than when he started his dental practice. She was relieved that Frank could now take charge of some of his father's patients. In the Adirondack Mountains of New York State, Dr. Edward Trudeau was already treating tubercular patients with plenty of fresh air, anticipating the opening of his sanatorium at Saranac Lake in 1884. In 1883, the Hospital for Sick Children opened a special hospital, called the Lakeside Home for Little Children, on Toronto Island for the treatment of young tubercular patients.[14] The sanatorium in Muskoka lay in the future, but some tubercular sufferers were going there to benefit from the clean air and higher elevation. Emily and John decided they should look for suitable property in Muskoka to purchase for a cottage site. Then John could spend as much time as he wished, away from the city.

A year earlier, the German physician and bacteriologist, Robert Koch, had isolated the tubercle bacillus. He introduced tuberculin for the treatment of the disease, but it proved to be ineffective. Tuberculin was later found to be useful in identifying individuals who carried live TB germs, but who as yet showed no signs of the disease. The 1880s have been called the era of the "bacteriological revolution."[15] Bacteriologists confirmed the germ theory of disease, but their research also showed that a clean environment alone, as claimed by the advocates of the sanitary idea, would not necessarily prevent disease. During the decade scientific research, rather than clinical observation, was found to be necessary if the causes of diseases were to be fully understood. Clinical application of the discoveries, however, for the most part lay in the future.

While scientists were realising the shortcomings of the sanitary idea, the City of Toronto finally took a positive step towards the improvement of public health and promotion of preventive medicine. Council set up a Board of Health and appointed a permanent, salaried, Medical Health Officer in place of temporary appointees. The man the city fathers chose was Dr. William Canniff, a native of Thurlow Township, Hastings County. Canniff was a graduate of the old Victoria College Faculty of Medicine and had received training in the United States and Britain. He is best remembered for his many historical writings, which included a history of the medical profession in Canada up to 1850. He had practised medicine in Belleville from 1864 to 1869, moving to Toronto in 1870 to succeed John Rolph (who died later in the year) as Dean of the Victoria Medical School. As chairman of the Canadian Medical Association's committee on vital statistics and public hygiene, Canniff had convinced the federal government to fund the collection of mortality statistics. In his new office he favoured persuasion, and a gradual education of politicians, rather than coercion. His approach was not unlike Dr. Emily Stowe's in her campaign for the advancement of women. Yet by contrast, where Emily found the city fathers co-operative, whatever their motives might have been, Canniff found his measures neither readily accepted nor enforced.[16]

With the establishment of a Medical Health Officer paid from the public purse, the city fathers had a new responsibility, and they hesitated to commit funds when they were answerable to an electorate with an eye on the mill rate. For herself, Emily was gratified at Canniff's appointment, but she continued to leave advances in the field of public health to the male doctors, while she gave leadership in improving the lot of women. Her goal remained the franchise; if they could achieve that single objective, women would gain more than if they dissipated their energies on too many other social causes.

By May 1883, Augusta Stowe and her fiancé, John Gullen, had qualified to practise medicine. Augusta's certificate from the Council of the College of Physicians and Surgeons of Ontario was dated the twenty-sixth of April, 1883. It was signed by "Jno. L. Bray, President," and Walter B. Geikie, Vice-President, and Robert Allan Pyne, Registrar. A handwritten note with the certificate states that Augusta interned during part of each of the four years that she was a medical student. John Gullen's certificate is preserved with Augusta's, as well as his diploma in Latin from the Trinity Medical College.[17] Augusta's degree, from Victoria College was M.D., while John's, from the University of Toronto was M.B. (In 1930 the University of Toronto changed the title of the degree to M.D.)

Augusta became the first woman doctor trained in Canada; Elizabeth Smith and the two other women who had entered Queen's in 1880 would not qualify until 1884. Emily had shown foresight in discouraging Augusta from entering the classes at Queen's that had been set up for women in the summer of 1880. Afterwards the women students were allowed to attend classes with the men.

The brave experiment at Queen's was short-lived. The male medical students objected to the presence of women in their classes, and they threatened to leave Queen's for Trinity. Unable to sustain the loss of the fees paid, Queen's capitulated in the face of this early demonstration of student power, and agreed not to accept any more women medical students. If women were to continue to train as doctors in Kingston, there would have to be an entirely separate school for them.[19] In Toronto, Drs. Stowe and Trout were still discussing, with Dr. Barrett and others, plans for a medical college for women. First, however, the Stowes were preoccupied with plans for the wedding of the two new doctors, Augusta Stowe, M.D., and John Gullen, M.B.

EIGHT

Stowe versus Trout — Two Medical Colleges

THE YEAR 1883 WAS one of achievement and great satisfaction for Emily Stowe, both in her private and public lives. On the twenty-third of May her daughter Augusta married John Gullen at the dignified, yellow-brick Metropolitan Methodist Church on Queen Street East. Reverend Hugh Johnson performed the ceremony and the reception followed at the home of the bride's parents, 111 Church Street. The young couple planned to go to New York City to take a course in children's diseases, but exactly when they worked this in is uncertain. Augusta's convocation at Victoria College, in Cobourg, did not take place until late in July, when the graduates from the Montreal *école* could arrive. Both events, the wedding and the convocation, received wide coverage in the Toronto press.

The Stowes were becoming celebrities. At the convocation in Cobourg, Dr. William Ogden, a professor at the Toronto School of Medicine, spoke proudly of Augusta as the first woman to be granted a medical degree in Canada. He recalled the occasion when some of the male students threatened to cause a disturbance, but the majority sided with Augusta. Afterwards, Dr. William Aikins, the President of the Toronto School of Medicine, gave the address to the graduates.[1]

Emily had to sandwich the wedding and the convocation between other vital activities. She was busy with plans for a medical college for women that would open in the autumn. She was still on the committee that had among its members Dr. Michael Barrett and Dr. Jenny Trout. Although Jenny had retired and her Electrotherapeutic Institute had lost money, the Trouts were still well off. Jenny volunteered to give an endowment towards the medical college, and offered an initial $10,000, but with certain conditions attached. She stated that she would donate this sum only if women sat on the governing board, and if women were appointed to the staff. Women, Dr. Trout insisted, should run a women's medical college. This led to a violent argument. Dr. Barrett was opposed, and for practical reasons. Where would they find enough qualified women in time to open the college that autumn? Emily, all her pent-up resentment of Jenny Trout boiling to the surface, sided with Dr. Barrett. Dr. Trout left the meeting in a huff. The next thing Emily heard was that Jenny had turned her eyes towards Kingston and Queen's, where the attempt to integrate women into classes with men was about to fail. Because of opposition from the male students, no more women would be admitted once the three then registered at the Royal College of Physicians and Surgeons in Kingston had graduated.

Queen's was only too happy to accept Dr. Trout's offer of funding. A separate college was a necessity if women were to be trained in the professions. The university called a meeting for June eighth, 1883, in the Kingston City Hall. Plans went ahead for a medical college to open in Kingston that autumn. Yet Jenny had been too impatient. On the eleventh the academics of the Toronto committee relented and agreed to allow women to join the governing body and staff of their intended college. Although the problem of finding qualified female staff remained, they had yielded to a principle.

A further meeting, organized by Emily Stowe and the Toronto Women's Suffrage Association, took place on the thirteenth of June at Shaftsbury House, the headquarters of the YMCA on King Street opposite Knox Church, to make a firm commitment to the setting up of the college that autumn. Edward Trout attended, and when he rose to defend Jenny the verbal exchanges grew quite heated. Edward accused the Toronto committee of being "copycat" and rude to the people of Kingston. He claimed the latter had delayed their plans until they thought there was no chance of a medical college in Toronto.

With Kingston going ahead, a medical school would not be needed in Toronto. There were not enough applicants to make both medical schools viable.[2] Nevertheless, the meeting passed the resolution, that "Medical education for women is a necessity and facilities for such should be provided."[3] As neither party would back down, two medical colleges for women would open in the autumn of 1883.

At the height of the bickering, John Stowe and his elder son Howard went off to Muskoka, following a lead that some delightful islands in Lake Joseph were for sale. Howard selected one, known as Crane Island, which belonged to Samuel and Margaret Crane, while John found one near Hamil's Point. Because Howard had no plan to build on Crane Island for some years, he agreed to switch with his father. John wanted to build soon, and Crane Island was closer to existing transportation. The property was registered to John Stowe on the thirtieth of August, 1883, for the sum of $50.00. John and Emily renamed it Stowe Island, and John set to work supervising the erection of a cottage.[4]

John would be able to spend as much time as he wished away from the city. In later years the family remembered that he usually left for Lake Joseph early each spring, remaining there until well into the fall. Two weeks after the property was registered, John's father died in Mount Pleasant. The family journeyed there for the funeral. John Stowe Sr. was buried in the Methodist cemetery beside a son, Jonas, who had died in 1855 at age twelve.

Meanwhile, viable or not, the enthusiasts in Toronto and in Kingston proceeded with their plans for the two medical colleges for women. Augusta and her husband John returned from their course in New York City. Augusta, now calling herself Dr. Stowe Gullen, accepted an appointment as demonstrator in anatomy at the embryo Toronto college. The Ontario Medical College for Women opened in rented premises at 291 Sumach Street, Toronto, in a small house with a crabapple tree in front and a lean-to at the back. To begin with, the only equipment was a skeleton.[5] In her pamphlet "A Brief History of the Ontario Medical College for Women," Augusta later recorded that Dr. Barrett was the college's first dean. The college committee consisted of:

Rev. John King, D.D.

Dr. James Carlyle

James Beatty, Q.C., M.P.

Professor Michael Barrett

Mrs. John Miller

Mrs. James Gooderham

Mrs. A.V. Lauder

Mrs. S.F. McMaster

Mrs. Donald McEwan

James Beatty, Q.C., M.P., chaired the board of trustees. The other trustees were:

Rev. Principal [William] Caven [of Victoria College]

Dr. Adam Wright [professor of obstetrics at Toronto School of Medicine]

Dr. Irving Cameron

Mrs. John Harris

Mrs. McEwan, secretary.

The first faculty members, in addition to Dr. Barrett, were

George Wright, M.A, M.B., Practice of Medicine

Irving H. Cameron, M.B., Surgery

Adam H. Wright, B.A., M.B., M.R.C.S. England, Obstetrics, Diseases of Women and Children

A. McPhedran, M.B., Materia Medica and Botany

J.T. Duncan, M.B., Anatomy and Microscopy

R.A. Reeve, B.S., M.D., Diseases of the Eye and Ear

R.B. Nevitt, B.A., M.D., Sanitary Science

Augusta Stowe Gullen, M.D., Demonstrator in Anatomy

F. Krauss, M.B., Medical Jurisprudence and Toxicology

A.R. Pyne, M.D., Chemistry.[6]

The first session opened on the first of October, 1883, with three students. As at the New York Medical College for Women that Emily had attended, all staff members were part-time.

In Kingston, meanwhile, the rival medical college for women commenced operations on the second of October in rooms offered at City Hall. Funds had been raised by private subscription, but the largest contributor was Dr. Jenny Trout. The college board asked to be affiliated with Queen's on the same terms as the Royal College for men. The first graduates were the three women who had started their medical training at the Royal College.[7] Once their own college opened, Elizabeth Smith, Alice McGillivray and Elizabeth Robb were only too happy to join it. Edward Trout's prediction that there would not be sufficient applicants to fill both medical colleges for women proved eventually to be true. The medical college at Queen's remained open until the session of 1893-1894, when the students were informed that that session would be the last. Students who had not completed their training could transfer to the Ontario Medical College for Women in Toronto.[8]

The medical colleges at both Kingston and Toronto had women among the governors, but Augusta Stowe Gullen was the first woman on a medical staff. While the Kingston college had no women on staff, it had six on the board of trustees, among them Dr. Jenny Trout. In addition to her original contribution of $10,000, Jenny endowed a scholarship of $50.00 a year. Yet Jenny lacked the endurance that characterized Emily Stowe, and the once prominent Dr. Trout sank into obscurity. The Trouts had no children, although they later adopted two. Augusta proudly carried on the fight her mother had started for women's rights, and kept her memory in the limelight, but little was heard of Jenny and her family after they moved to Scarborough in 1887.[9]

December of 1883 saw a second marriage in the Stowe household, one that was not as widely reported as the first. Emily's elder son, Howard, now aged twenty-two, married Belle St. Croix.[10] Howard was listed in the *Toronto Directory* as a clerk with Paterson Brothers, "bds. 111 Church." At first Howard and his wife lived with the family. By 1884, Augusta and John Gullen were living at 238 Spadina Avenue. The following year Howard Stowe was a traveller for S.F. McKinnon and Company, and renting rooms at 238 Spadina Avenue from his sister and brother-in-law.

Early in 1884, Emily was gratified by further evidence that her struggle for the cause was succeeding. The Ontario Legislature voted, by order-in-council, to admit women to the 1884-1885 session at the University of Toronto. Her boast to Dr. McCaul back in 1853 had not been idle. She had told him she would see that the doors of the university were opened one day to women; the hours she had spent collecting signatures for the petition had been well spent. Great-uncle Solomon Lossing had shown her the way. Persistence paid off. In October 1884, nine women entered University College as undergraduates, and in June 1885, five received Bachelor of Arts degrees, four with honours in modern languages, and one in classics.[11] Women were still not admitted to the Toronto School of Medicine (Augusta's had been an exceptional case) nor to the Trinity Medical College, but that did not matter now. Women could enrol in the Ontario Medical College for Women where, Emily was confident, they would soon show that they could do at least as well as, and most likely better than their male counterparts.

Women were gaining more opportunities in the field of medicine through improvements in the education of nurses. Now that nursing had become a more respectable calling, and as the number of nursing schools grew, women had that choice open to them. Nursing as a career had Emily's blessing; it was truly within woman's sphere. She encouraged women to enter the new schools of nursing, whose academic requirements were less stringent than the medical college. At the same time, Emily was promoting enrollment in the Ontario Medical College for Women; trained nurses complemented doctors, although they should not replace them, except perhaps in remote areas where doctors were not available.

She applauded the efforts of Dr. William Canniff, the new Medical Health Officer, in his drive to clean up Toronto. Canniff was an enthusiast for "the sanitary idea." He had five policemen going from door to door surveying the condition of houses and their back yards. Canniff favoured a city water supply to replace wells contaminated by nearby privies. By an amendment to the Public Health Act of 1884, the Medical Health Officer was empowered to look into schools, factories and homes, and to inspect food and noxious trades. Through newspapers he promoted cleanliness and public awareness of health hazards. In 1883, his first year as Medical Health Officer, his office had received 500 complaints and the numbers had risen each year. (By 1889 this number would reach 6,000.)[12] Various proposals were placed before council for improvements to the city waterworks and for a trunk sewer. Water, drawn from Lake Ontario, was still fairly pure although a sewer that ran along King Street emptied into Toronto Bay. The Toronto Sanitary Association, formed in 1884, was an organization in which the Toronto Women's Suffrage Association took a great interest while holding the franchise as its main goal. Emily often alluded to the need for cleanliness in her lectures, but she warned that women should not spread themselves too thin. Let Dr. Canniff give leadership in the fight for a trunk sewer and a municipal water supply; for Emily her sights were on the single objective of women's suffrage.

By 1885, the women's movement in Toronto had gained a valuable male ally in the person of Mr. John Waters, Liberal Member of the Ontario Legislature for North Middlesex. As a Liberal he was not a member of the opposition, the logical place to find support, but of Oliver Mowat's own government. Waters introduced his first bill proposing provincial woman suffrage, at the same time warning the house that "he would introduce a woman suffrage bill in every session until he got it passed, or as long as he sat in the House." He would be true to his promise; over the next eight years he was to sponsor nine "measures." At times he asked that the municipal franchise be extended to married women; at others, his plea was for the provincial franchise for married women. For the most part the members greeted his speeches with laughter, because even men of his own party treated his efforts as a joke.[13]

Unfortunately, by the time Waters lent his support, the Toronto Women's Suffrage Association was in a temporary slump. The reason for this loss of momentum is not readily apparent. Perhaps some members were satisfied with the gains they had made thus far, or others were discouraged. Neither of these reasons would have applied to Dr. Emily Stowe, the vigour of whose leadership was flagging. Perhaps she had had to pay more attention to her practice. More likely, she was spending considerable time with her husband John. By now he lived half the year on Stowe Island in Muskoka, where he felt healthier than in the city. He had retired, handing over the entire practice to his son, Frank. The original cottage on the island was now flanked by small guest cabins for the growing family and the many friends. Whenever Emily could see the way clear she, too, was spending time on Stowe Island, to give John in return the support he had long given her. She may have guessed that their time together was limited, and decided to be with him while both were still fit enough to do things together.

In 1885, the Stowes suffered another bereavement. John's mother, Alice, died in Mount Pleasant. She was buried in the Methodist cemetery next to her husband, John Stowe Sr. and Jonas, their son.[14]

An important development in Emily's profession was the establishment, in 1886, by the Sisters of St. John the Divine, of St. John's Women's Surgical Hospital.[15] Both Emily and Augusta would be welcomed on the floors of St. John's, and in the operating theatres. Now that hospitals were becoming more important in the practice of medicine the women were gratified to have a facility where they could be certain of a warm reception. At that time Emily and John were expecting their first grandchild. On the twenty-sixth of May, Howard's wife Belle gave birth to a daughter whom they named Emily, after her grandmother.

While Emily was concentrating on her personal affairs, the voters of Toronto elected a reform council under Mayor William Howland. Emily suspected the votes of the single women were sufficient to change the balance of power. The new council soon passed a bylaw to regulate slaughterhouses, a sound step in the field of public health. Now Medical Health Officer William Canniff was asking that foul wells and privies in the downtown area be closed, and that funds be provided to build the trunk sewer. He had some support from the new council, but even reform members dug their toes in as they contemplated the enormous cost of such a project, estimated at more than a million dollars, an unimaginable sum for a municipality to spend at that time.[16]

The same year some homeopathic practitioners decided to found a hospital. They started with a dispensary on Richmond Street East, and Emily was welcomed within its walls. (Later the hospital moved to Jarvis Street.)[17]

Another event of great interest to Emily was the establishment, in

1887, by an act of the legislature, of the Faculty of Medicine of the University of Toronto. The university became a teaching body for the first time since the Hincks Act of 1853. In preparation for this development, the Minister of Education, the Honourable George W. Ross, held discussions with the Toronto School of Medicine, which agreed to become the medical faculty. Ross had hoped that the Trinity Medical College would amalgamate with the new Faculty of Medicine, but the dean of the Trinity school, Walter B. Geikie, declined on the grounds that elimination of the competition that had long existed between the two rivals would lead to a decline in the quality of medical education. That year, Victoria University joined in federation with the University of Toronto. The medical *école* for francophones in Montreal closed down soon afterwards.[18] (Victoria remained in Cobourg until 1892, when the university resolved to move to Toronto to its present site on Queen's Park Crescent, adjacent to the main University of Toronto campus.)

For some time Emily's contacts with her old home in Norwich had been tenuous. In 1888 they almost came to an end with the death of her mother, Hannah Howard Jennings. Mrs. Jennings, then seventy-nine years old, died in New York City while staying with her fifth daughter, Dr. Hannah Kimball. The body was brought to Toronto to be buried in Mount Pleasant Cemetery beside her husband, Solomon, after a short memorial service in the house at 111 Church Street. A "token of remembrance" that Peter Lossing, Hannah's grandfather, had composed in 1826, and Hannah's death notice were preserved by the family.[19]

Emily's youngest sister, Ella Jennings, was still a busy doctor in New York City. Like Emily, Ella was in demand as a lecturer. One of her topics was "The Effect of Alcohol Upon the Human System from a Physician's Stand Point."[20]

Emily Stowe's period of inactivity in the quest for the vote ended in 1888 with the news of an important development. In many countries women were forming local and national councils. Women planned to gather in Washington, D.C., for a great congress of the central body of the newly constituted International Council of Women. All over the world women had started to unite, and Emily wanted to ensure that women in her country were not left behind. Although John was no stronger, he encouraged Emily to return to the battlefield to revitalize the Toronto Women's Suffrage Association. She prepared to attend the Congress of the International Council of Women, as the representative of the Toronto suffragists. Bessie Starr Keefer would represent the Women's Christian Temperance Union, while the Toronto women, Mrs. Mary Macdonnell and Mrs. Emily Willoughby Cummings, would also be delegates. Two other women from unspecified parts of the country were to go, making in all six delegates. The records of this congress, attended also by such women as Emily's old friend Susan Anthony, are sparse.[21] Whatever went on, Emily returned to Toronto convinced that more Canadian women and their organisations ought to attend the second congress. The International Council of Women resolved to hold the congress every five years, the next one in 1893. Emily would need all the intervening time to ensure a good representation.

NINE

Death of John Stowe

AT THE INTERNATIONAL CONGRESS of Women that met in Washington in 1888, Emily renewed her acquaintance with Elizabeth Cady Stanton. Susan Anthony and Mrs. Stanton and their supporters stood for the federal franchise for women. The group led by Lucy Stone and Henry Ward Beecher favoured a more gradual approach, picking off one state after another. By 1890, the two factions had united into one strong National American Woman Suffrage Association, to advance the cause at both state and federal levels. Inspired by the convention of 1888, Emily Stowe revived her enthusiasm for the cause and contacted women who had been active up to 1885. Again, as when she started the Toronto Women's Literary Club, Emily conducted meetings at the Stowe house on Church Street.

The members of the Toronto Women's Suffrage Association invited the remarkable American, Anna Howard Shaw, whom Emily had met in Washington, to address a gathering. Shaw was an ordained "Methodist Protestant" minister who had obtained a medical degree from Boston in 1886. She was well known to New England suffragists like Lucy Stone, but she had only become acquainted with Susan Anthony at the International Council of Women in Washington in 1888. The Reverend Shaw, M.D., was also the superintendent of franchise of the Women's Christian Temperance Union in the United States.[1] The meeting took place on the thirty-first of January, 1889, in what the press called Association Hall, in reality Shaftesbury Hall. "Association" referred to the YMCA; the name Shaftesbury was in honour of the British patron, Lord Shaftesbury. Emily and the friends on her committee had sent out 4,000 invitations to ensure the meeting would be a success. The hall was crowded, with men as well as women.

Dr. Shaw, who appeared to be a lady of considerable "force of character and confidence," was a facile speaker. Her theme stressed the importance of enfranchising women for the benefit of the community. Women were more religious than men and would bring morality to government. Women were thriftier than men, for men wasted in cigars what a woman would spend on a bonnet. Votes for women would assure man's "elevation and improvement." The very nature of woman suited her to vote and, furthermore, men made poor representatives for women. Men did not use their votes intelligently, and not all men were even interested in casting their votes. Dr. Shaw maintained that "woman should find her own place in government, in society, at home and everywhere." The chairman presiding was James Beatty, Q.C., the first chairman of the board of trustees for the Ontario Medical College for Women. Beatty, a true friend of women's rights, had also been a member of the legislature in 1883 when single women received the right to vote in municipal elections. Before the meeting broke up the participants had passed a resolution that all taxpaying citizens should be enfranchised.[2]

In the wave of enthusiasm that followed Dr. Shaw's visit, Emily was able to revive the old Toronto Women's Suffrage Association but on a grander, nation-wide scale, as the Dominion Women's Enfranchisement Association. Emily was elected the first president, a post she held the rest of her life. During the year that followed, other cities and towns in Ontario formed their own branches of the new organisation.[3]

Emily and her supporters in the Dominion Women's Enfranchisement Association now saw the merit in unity among all women. They were preparing a deputation to the Ontario Legislature to urge the passage of John Waters' latest bill, to enfranchise all widows and spinsters for provincial elections. For Emily, the bill did not go far enough, but its passage would be a step forward and better than nothing. On previous occasions the suffragists had approached the elected representatives on their own, but this time they acted in co-operation with the Women's Christian Temperance Union. Each sent a delegation, while hundreds more women waited outside the House. Emily spoke on their behalf, and was careful to reassure her audience that women were not anxious to displace any existing minister:

> We are not office seekers, and do not wish to take from those
> in power, any well-merited crown, but we do as educated
> citizens, as moral and loving women, desire to be placed in a
> position to impress directly our thought upon our nation and
> times....If the women of our country are not all prepared to
> use the newly imposed responsibility intelligently neither are
> men prepared to use it intelligently. Of this I am certain, that
> the women of our country desire to use it only for their
> country's good [4]

Premier Mowat (who was also his own Attorney General) listened "sphinx-like" according to one reporter, then made his customary assurances of sympathy to the women's cause. He quite agreed with what Emily had said. *But* he was a practical politician, and he could not see how the women could get their wish. Emily, furious with Mowat, managed to keep control of her temper at the time. Later, she found release by waxing caustic in the press. The bill was defeated on its second reading. Despite all his honeyed words and feigned sympathy, Mowat had voted with those who defeated the bill. In an article in the *Globe*, Emily suggested that Mowat be "less the politician and more the Christian."[5] If Mowat was held up as an example of a Christian man, small wonder that Emily had become a free-thinker.

In May she delivered her lecture on "Housewifery," an expression she often used, to stress the significance of the home. Homemaking was:

> ... the most important and far reaching in its effects upon
> humanity." Woman should be as free to choose her vocation
> as man, "tethered by no conventionalities, enslaved by no
> chains either of her own or man's forging.
> No trade, profession or calling demands more versatility of

talent and unwearying industry and watchfulness. The woman who is an adept in this art of housewifery in its broadest sense merits the highest respect and commendation of all her sister women .... The statesman is assisted by his peer, and here let me say that governing a state is merely keeping house on a large scale .... Political economy and domestic economy bear a striking resemblance to each other.[6]

She recalled going into badly managed homes of women who had never been taught housewifery. Too many young women started married life without suitable training. They had gone out to work as mere children, and had no idea how to care for a home when they married.

The year ended with two events close to Emily's heart. In November her second son, Frank, married Miss Mary Gibbs Hudson, a daughter of the financier, Rufus Sawyer Hudson (known to his associates as R.S.). The ceremony took place in the Jarvis Street Baptist Church, where the Hudson family were members. The couple began their married life at 111 Church Street, where Frank still had his office, sharing the space with Emily and with John when he came home from Muskoka. John stayed on Stowe Island well into the late fall, where the fresh air, no matter how cold, seemed to be good for him.

After Frank's wedding Emily, as a delegate for the Dominion Women's Enfranchisement Association, attended the Women's Christian Temperance Union convention in Joliet, Illinois. She probably took a steamer across Lake Ontario and travelled on by train through Chicago. Although the purpose of the convention was to reduce the consumption of alcohol, the women reached a consensus that their objective would be advanced more rapidly if they had political power. Having agreed on this point, the delegates proceeded to establish a Women's Protective Association in the United States so that women who were abused or exploited would have somewhere to turn. Emily approved of this measure and hoped to see a similar organization set up in Canada.[7]

On the second of December, Susan Anthony came to Toronto; she was one of several guest lecturers the Dominion Women's Enfranchisement Association had engaged. The address Miss Anthony presented before a very large audience of men and women was favourably reported in the press. She stated that "disenfranchisement always meant not only political degradation but social, moral and industrial degradation as well." [8] Emily was delighted to have in her own city the famous American suffragist whom she had first met in New York City in 1866 while studying under Dr. Clemence Lozier.

The Dominion Women's Enfranchisement Association was now in need of a paid executive. At a meeting with Emily in the chair, the members selected Mrs. Mary Seymour Howell, of Albany, New York, because she was a competent organiser and effective lecturer. Mrs. Howell travelled throughout Ontario setting up more branches, and Emily, too, travelled considerable distances, lecturing and handing out pamphlets and other reading material on women's rights. At one lecture to women in Toronto in January, 1890, Emily proposed a ship canal to link Lake Ontario by way of the Humber River, through Lake Simcoe and on to Georgian Bay.[9] On the tenth of March, 1890, she addressed an open letter to the Mayor of Toronto, Edward Frederick Clarke, spelling out the pitfalls of maintaining separate polling booths for men and women:

> If men and women can be companions in life, associate in the home, at the fireside, sit side by side at the same table, in church, in places of instruction and amusement, also in the street and steam cars, in the name of common sense and economy I ask what apology can be offered for separate polling booths for women?

The extra booths were not only a needless waste of money, but they might give dishonest male scrutineers the opportunity to interfere with women's ballots if they could be identified. Since the women's ballots would be in separate boxes, tampering with their votes would be a simple matter.[10]

She was soon castigating the Reverend M.C. Lockwood because he neglected the women workers in a speech he made on labour unrest. Her article was headlined, "A Woman's Protest. Dr. Lockwood Speaks only to Men, an Open Letter to Dr. Lockwood." He offered not a word of pity over an unsuccessful strike some women staged, although he was very sympathetic to men strikers. Woman's cause was the same as man's. Emily rejected the oft-stated and erroneous reply that women were not enfranchised because they did not ask to be, or that they had told Parliament:

We *don't want* the franchise — we want bread! My heart bleeds for the disenfranchised women of every land, and when I hear a man like yourself ignoring the rights and claims of one half of God's people to an equal freedom and co-operation in building up *this new*, more just and equitable society — that can never be built without woman's best and fullest cooperation — I am constrained in the fullness of my heart to cry aloud and say, 'How long, Oh Lord, how long, must thy servants endure this hateful bondage?'" [11]

By June, Emily and her workers had organized the first Dominion Conference of the Enfranchisement Association. Delegates arrived in Toronto from branches across the country. Most were from Ontario, but a few branches that had sprung up in the larger cities of the west and east sent representatives. Among those from the United States were Reverend Dr. Anna Shaw and Dr. Hannah Kimball, M.D., Emily's sister. The newspapers did not report where the meetings took place on the twelfth and thirteenth, but the hall was decorated with posters bearing slogans such as "Canada's Daughters Should be Free," "No Sex in Citizenship," and "Women are Half the People." Before the meetings ended, the delegates had re-elected Emily president of the association.

In her address as president, Emily observed that the movement was well-founded despite criticisms that woman suffrage would lead to free love and more Bloomer girls. To women who, she feared, thought the franchise was "unbiblical" she offered reassurances. "God had declared it was not well for man to be alone, but man had assumed to be wiser than God and in the matter of Government had worked alone." [12]

Emily's message was aimed at a group of women who held an opposing point of view, few of whom would have attended the convention but who would follow the newspaper reports. They believed that women did not need the vote; their role was to educate their sons and influence their husbands to use the franchise wisely. A leader who held this point of view was Mrs. John Hoodless of Hamilton. Born Adelaide Hunter on a farm at St. George, Ontario, in 1857, Mrs. Hoodless was a contemporary of Augusta Stowe Gullen's. In future, Mrs. Hoodless's objectives would sometimes coincide with Emily's; in general, both women wanted the same reforms, but their methods were different.[13]

While the women were holding their convention, a provincial medical convention was also taking place in Toronto. Each convention sent courteous greetings to the other, but the doctors were careful not to endorse woman suffrage; some, according to one newspaper report, made sarcastic comments. Dr. Hannah Kimball sent a reply rebutting any suggestions that ladies, for any reason, might destroy the foundations of public morality.[14]

Emily was riding a crest and was pleased with the momentum the women's movement had acquired in the past two years. The association had an invaluable ally in the Women's Christian Temperance Union, and the churches were gradually coming over to the women's side. In an official bulletin, the Methodist Church admitted, "If women were allowed to vote more rapid progress would be made in dealing legislatively with the evils arising from traffic in intoxicating drinks."[15]

The Ontario Medical College for Women was a success and enrolment was expanding. By 1890 it had outgrown the house on Sumach Street, and the board had arranged to purchase a building on Sackville Street. At that time Miss Anna McFee, in her last year as a medical student at the College, was instrumental in starting a clinic where women physicians treated women patients who, because they were too modest to consult male doctor, were neglecting their health. At first the clinics were general, but soon they were divided into medicine, obstetrics and gynæcology.[16]

Before the year ended, Emily, John, Frank and his wife Mary, moved farther north on Church Street, from 111 to 119. Augusta Stowe Gullen and her husband John left 238 Spadina Avenue and purchased number 461 on the same street. Howard Stowe, his wife Belle and four-year-old daughter Emily left 238 Spadina and settled into a house he purchased at 9 North Street. Emily and John may have rented the house at 111 Church Street, but they purchased number 119. The same year, Dr. William Canniff resigned as Medical Health Officer.

After seven years of diplomacy and negotiating with the politicians, both at City Hall and at the legislature, Canniff felt he had done his duty, although he had realised few of his objectives. He retired to write local histories, especially his magnum opus on the settlement of Upper Canada for which he is now better known than as a medical health officer. His successor for two years was Dr. Norman Allen, who was followed in 1893 by Dr. Charles Sheard.[17]

As 1891 opened Emily saw a fresh triumph. The Women's Christian Temperance Union made the momentous decision to endorse women's suffrage. This added considerable weight to the aspirations of the Dominion Women's Enfranchisement Association. Yet her elation was tempered by the knowledge that she would not have her husband much longer. Helpless in spite of her training, she watched John failing day by day. With other patients and their families she had often tried to instil hope when she knew there was none. With John she had to face the truth. He was only sixty years old, but with his background of tuberculosis Emily felt fortunate to have had him as long as she did. And yet, when the end came, in December, Emily was relieved that he would no longer suffer.

After a funeral service at the house, John was buried in Mount Pleasant Cemetery near Solomon and Hannah Jennings. Also that year, Emily's third sister, Paulina (1838-1891), the wife of John Duncan (1830-1892), died at fifty-three. Paulina was the first of the six Jennings sisters to die.

Mourning was a luxury Emily could not afford. So much had to be done, and being busy would help her overcome her loss. She had more invitations to lecture than she could accept. Considerable promotional and administrative work had to be done for the enfranchisement association, and she had to attend to her still substantial medical practice.

Developments in the field of health care were a constant source of interest. The Toronto General Hospital was no longer adequate to meet the demands of the expanding city. John Gullen was on a committee promoting a second general hospital, and Augusta was helping him, while the Sisters of St. Joseph were planning to open St. Michael's

Hospital the following season. The students at the Ontario Medical College for Women had privileges at most of the hospitals, but they were to have exclusive privileges at St. Michael's.[18]

Howard and Belle's little Emily was a source of joy to her grandmother, while Frank and Mary's first child was born on the fourth of May, 1891, a second granddaughter, named Edith Nylita Stowe.[19] Augusta and John Gullen had no children, perhaps from choice. Augusta seemed content with teaching, her busy practice, interest in woman suffrage and local politics, and an active social life. Because of a stately bearing and the latest fashion in clothes, many people who saw photographs of Augusta taken while she was a young woman assumed that she put up with constricting corsets in the interest of high fashion. One newspaper opinion indicates she did not tolerate corsets for long. Dr. Augusta Stowe Gullen walked so well because her skirts fell from her shoulders and allowed the full use of the muscles around her waist. More women ought to emulate her, and "let out the strings that make your noses red and your eyes stare."[20]

By 1892, women were eligible to stand for the Toronto School Board. Augusta was elected in the 4th Ward. Her keen common sense and pragmatism served her well at meetings where she was, naturally, the defender of women teachers. Any suggestion of a cut in their salaries roused her ire, especially when the trustees did not propose a corresponding cut for men teachers. When Trustee Bell moved to have the wearing of bloomers by lady teachers reported to the board on the grounds that the garments were immoral, Augusta was quick to respond. Women who wore bloomers, Bell announced, were prostitutes. On her feet even before Bell had finished, Augusta demanded that he speak like a gentleman. She retorted that she herself had worn the costume "as a child," and it was not immoral. Bell's motion was defeated by a vote of thirteen to six.[21]

Early in the new year Emily and her son Frank with his wife Mary purchased 463 Spadina Avenue, next door to Augusta and John Gullen, and leased 119 Church Street. Emily, Frank and Mary needed the new house to relieve the sorrow associated with 119 Church. For Emily, the house had too many memories of John, while Frank and Mary had suffered their own bereavement when, on the twenty-sixth of January, 1893, their daughter Edith died, aged nineteen months.[22] Mary's impending second labour in March was more a cause for worry than happiness. Marie Augusta Stowe was born on the fifteenth, to be watched anxiously by parents whose confidence had been undermined by the loss of their firstborn.

Once they were settled, Emily ordered new business cards to announce that she had removed from 119 Church Street to 463 Spadina, informing her patients, "Belt Line cars pass the office; telephone 3045."[23]

She was now preparing to attend the World's Fair in Chicago, scheduled for May, 1893. The proper name was the World's Columbian Exposition, to commemorate Columbus Day, the twelfth of October, 1892, when the site was dedicated. The second convention of the International Congress of Women would be held in conjunction with the great exposition. The delegates from the Dominion Women's Enfranchisement Association were Dr. Emily Stowe, Mrs. Sarah Ann Curzon, Dr. Augusta Stowe Gullen and Mrs. Ida Taylor Scales. Among others planning to attend were the Toronto journalist Mrs Emily Willoughby Cummings, and Mrs. Mary Macdonnell. [24]

TEN

Emily and Ishbel

THE QUINQUENNIAL CONVENTION of the International Congress of Women opened at the Chicago World's Fair in May, 1893. A pamphlet entitled "World's Congress of Representative Women" reported that in addition to four ladies from the Dominion Women's Enfranchisement Association other Canadian organizations who sent delegations were the Dominion Branch of the International Order of King's Daughters, and the Canadian Congregation of the Women's Board of Missions. All told, some sixty Canadian women, from five different organizations, went to Chicago. Mrs. Adelaide Hoodless was one of the three delegates representing the Young Women's Christian Association.[1] Adelaide, who had been a founder member of the Hamilton branch of the YWCA, was a crusader for the introduction of domestic science into Ontario schools. Like Emily, Adelaide thought the assumption that girls would be taught homemaking by their mothers was erroneous; many mothers were incapable of instructing them. Mrs. Emily Willoughby Cummings also attended the conference in Chicago. Although a member of the Dominion Women's Enfranchisement Association, she was the representative of the Toronto branch of the YWCA.

Emily was delighted to be reunited with Susan Anthony and to meet other American suffragists whom she knew only through their correspondence. Most of the delegates were American, Canadian or

British, but an encouraging number of women from other countries, mostly European, had also made their way to Chicago. All were exultant that one state, Oregon, was to grant women the vote that same year.

Beginning at 11 a.m. on the fifteenth of May, the congress ran until the evening of the twenty-first of May and encompassed seventy-six sessions. More than 600 women participated, and well over 150,000 women and men attended.[2]

At a session on the nineteenth the women debated the choice of a president for the international organization, and they decided to request Lady Aberdeen to accept the office. Ishbel, Lady Aberdeen, was the wife of John Gordon, 7th Earl of Aberdeen. Ishbel was then thirty-six, Emily sixty-two. The choice was especially good for Canada. The Aberdeens had toured the Dominion twice, and had property in British Columbia. And Lord Aberdeen had just been appointed the next Governor General of Canada to succeed Lord Stanley who wanted to resign.[3]

The Aberdeens were in Chicago during the congress. His Lordship had been Viceroy of Ireland, and they had come to attend the Irish exhibit. Lady Aberdeen accepted the presidency of the International Council of Women with alacrity. Emily may have been among the Canadian delegates who met with her to discuss the formation of a National Council of Women of Canada. The Aberdeens were well-known Liberals, appointed to the Canadian post on the recommendation of the prime minister of Britain, William Ewart Gladstone. The Canadian suffragists soon formed the opinion that the formidable Ishbel might be just the person to shake up the Tory government in Ottawa, now headed by Sir John Thompson. No doubt women of Adelaide Hoodless's stripe were less thrilled; Lady Aberdeen was herself a suffragist.

Ishbel realized she had to tread the middle ground, between Doctors Stowe and Stowe Gullen with the other members of the Dominion Women's Enfranchisement Association, and the more conservative faction led by Mrs. Hoodless who did not believe that enfranchisement was necessary. The latter women preferred to devote their time to the promotion of domestic science training and to establishing safe hostels for working-class girls flocking to the cities from the farms in search of employment. Certainly, the work of the YWCA in taking care of young single women new to urban life was admirable, and Emily herself recognized its merits. But for Ishbel, women representatives of all worthy social causes had to be accommodated within a National Council of Women; unity was of utmost importance in achieving reforms.

Emily's mood was buoyant when, with other participants, she took her seat on a platform at one of the meetings. She did not notice that she was perilously close to the edge, and without warning she missed her footing and crashed to the floor below, unable to rise. A horse-drawn ambulance was summoned and, accompanied by Augusta she was taken to a local hospital. To her everlasting grief she had broken a hip, a disaster in 1893.[4] The only treatment prescribed was traction in bed, until, months later, doctors pronounced the break knitted.

Meanwhile, three delegates from each of the five Canadian organizations present, with other Canadian women in attendance, held a meeting. Adelaide Hoodless reported:

> Canada was the only country — representing advanced civilization — not officially represented through an official body of women .... There were only five Canadian organizations officially represented at the Congress, by the Dominion Women's Christian Temperance Union, the Young Women's Christian Association, the Missionary Society of Canada, the Dominion Order of King's Daughters and the Women's Enfranchisement Association ... the Canadian delegates called a meeting then and there to discuss forming a National Council of Canada.[5]

But for the accident the first president of the National Council of Women of Canada might have been Dr. Emily Stowe. Instead, Mrs. Mary Macdonnell was selected by the Canadian delegates and the other women present. Mrs. Emily Willoughby Cummings was selected as the first secretary. Of this lady, Ishbel wrote:

> [she] is a very nice little woman, Mrs. Cummings, a widow and a lady of good connection in Toronto. She was left very

badly off by her husband who died about a year ago and at present she is writing the weekly Woman's Page for 'The Globe'.[6]

Emily was still convalescent at home that October when the inaugural meeting of the National Council of Women of Canada convened in Toronto. Beforehand, Lady Aberdeen, now settled in Rideau Hall in Ottawa, agreed to accept the presidency. The meeting was held in the Horticultural Pavilion (now Allan Gardens) with Lady Aberdeen in the chair. Augusta was certainly there, but Emily probably did not attend. The accident in Chicago had slowed her down and was to lead to her early retirement from her medical practice. Yet she remained as active as her lameness and pain would allow in the cause of women's suffrage.

In March, 1894, the Dominion Women's Enfranchisement Association and the Women's Christian Temperance Union joined together to confront Premier Mowat, now Sir Oliver, at the Ontario Legislature. Again, they received the same polite sympathy but no assurances of action. This time, the delegation, 150 strong, was led by two men, F.S. Spence for those in favour, not just of temperance but of prohibition, and Dr. J.L. Hughes on behalf of the Dominion Women's Enfranchisement Association. Because Emily was still laid up, Dr. Augusta Stowe Gullen was on hand to deliver an address. But either through oversight or design, she was not given an opportunity to speak. Dr. Hughes left a copy of the address in the hope that some members of the government would be sufficiently interested to read it.[7]

By April, Emily was in better form and able to attend the first annual meeting of the National Council of Women of Canada, in Ottawa. At this meeting she had the opportunity to become acquainted with Adelaide Hoodless and to support her where their views coincided. Adelaide had lost a small son owing to contaminated milk, and both women were concerned with better methods of handling perishable foods. On the twelfth, Mrs. Hoodless read a paper on the need, in the public schools, for domestic science courses for girls and manual training for boys. When she proposed a motion that the national council do all in its power to further the introduction of such programmes, Emily rose and spoke in favour of its passing. As she had often done in her lecture on "Housewifery", she cited the frightful scenes she observed in too many homes while on her rounds to visit patients. These appalling conditions would not prevail if girls could study domestic science in schools. Lady Aberdeen added her weight in support: "We believe implicitly that the home is the woman's first mission."[8]

The motion passed, and the members voted to establish a standing committee on Domestic Science and Technical Training, with Mrs. Hoodless as the national convenor.[9]

For the next few years the suffragists were less active, some, no doubt, disenchanted. Emily was preoccupied with matters at home. She was still seeing patients, although Augusta and John Gullen carried the bulk of the clinical load. Her son Howard's wife, Belle, was not strong, and their little daughter, Emily, spent most of her time with her grandmother at 463 Spadina Avenue. When Belle died young, the child was so often at the Spadina house that the legend grew that Dr. Stowe had an adopted daughter named Emily. On the twenty-sixth of January, 1895, Frank and Mary's third daughter was born, and they named her Hilda Isobel Stowe. Now there were three granddaughters at 463 Spadina Avenue — Howard's Emily, Frank's Marie and Hilda. Had Frank's first daughter, Edith, lived, Emily's happiness as a grandmother would have been complete.

During the summer of 1895, Lord and Lady Aberdeen toured the maritime provinces and afterwards went to Victoria. When they returned in the autumn they stopped for a few days in Toronto on their way home to Rideau Hall. Ishbel paid a call on Dr. Emily Stowe that was duly reported in the press.[10]

The formation of branches of the National Council of Women, the lack of nurses and doctors in remote areas of the country, and the need to improve education were all subjects uppermost in the minds of both women. To Emily, improvement in education should benefit women and girls, but Lady Aberdeen had seen pioneer communities in the west where few even had books to read. While Augusta Stowe Gullen, on the school board, argued for better working conditions for women teachers in the City of Toronto, Ishbel arranged for parcels of books and magazines to be shipped to isolated villages and farms across the prairies and in the southern parts of British Columbia.

Ishbel had great hopes for the Liberal Party of Canada, which was certain to be more sympathetic to women than the Tories, despite the slow pace of reform by the Liberal government of Ontario. Emily wanted to press for enfranchisement, but Ishbel, while in favour, felt that all reforms required the same priority, if only to keep the goodwill of women like Mrs. Hoodless. Even without the franchise Ishbel felt women could accomplish much, whereas Emily remained steadfast to her central objective. Ishbel, too, would meet with opposition.

The two women had much in common; each held liberal views. Emily had given a lecture on the incongruity of making drunkenness a crime while the sale of alcohol was condoned. Both Emily and Ishbel preferred a humane approach to the treatment of criminals. They were less in accord on the matter of temperance. When she arrived in Canada, Ishbel found only two burning issues among women — temperance and the vote. Lady Aberdeen was not an abstainer like Emily, and was not sympathetic to the Women's Christian Temperance Union. She could work with the suffragists, but not to the exclusion of other reform groups. Like Emily, Ishbel approved of the Women's Protective Association but she was concerned that many factory girls were afraid to join it lest they be dismissed from their jobs. Lady Aberdeen gave the association the needed respectability by becoming its patron.[11]

By 1895, as promised in 1892, the Ontario Medical College for Women had its exclusive privileges at St. Michael's Hospital. Women doctors could also be assured of a welcome if they sought privileges in a new general hospital slated to open in 1896 in rented premises at 393-395 Manning Avenue. In 1895, it had opened as the Toronto Western Free Dispensary at 417 Euclid Avenue. Twelve doctors met in December and each agreed to pay one hundred dollars towards the maintenance of the Western Hospital, a further ten dollars down and five dollars per month. One of the founding doctors was John Gullen, assisted by his wife Augusta. This was the beginning of the Toronto Western Hospital, which eventually moved to its present site on Bathurst Street.[12]

The episode for which Emily Stowe the suffragist was most famous was the Mock Parliament of February, 1896. To arouse public awareness of the cause of women's rights, the Dominion Women's Enfranchisement Association, in cooperation with the Women's Christian Temperance Union, held what they called the Ontario Legislature of Women at the Horticultural Pavilion, in which sympathetic men also played a part. Opposition was not lacking. One newspaper wanted the City Council to forbid the women to use the Pavilion:

> I suspect this is but a deep-laid scheme for the new women to show that they are capable of filling legislative positions .... It would be simply dreadful if the Board of Control should ever come under the management of women.[13]

City Council paid no attention and the meeting went ahead; what was called a parliament of fifty of the strongest-minded women of Toronto sat in state. The report in the Toronto *Star* of 18 February began:

> The Women's Parliament was amusing — it afforded heaps of fun, as it was intended to do. Every woman present seemed to feel that here was her opportunity to express herself, to impress her individuality on the world. The tyrant — man — came in for a liberal share of denunciation. On the other hand he was well defended.[14]

Emily was the Attorney General (one of Sir Oliver Mowat's two hats). Augusta was the Minister of Crown Lands. Emily was also the honourable member for Oxford, while Augusta represented Brant.[15] Men friendly to the cause played the downtrodden members of the opposite sex who came humbly petitioning for the vote. Dr. Stowe, in a parody of Sir Oliver Mowat that brought the house down, dismissed them, saying that while she favoured "the right of the individual to representation in the Government to which he contributes and belongs," her colleagues prevented her taking action. She promised, in the best of political styles, to give their request serious consideration. The members used the same specious arguments they had heard on their appearances before the legislature.

A favourite bill presented was "An Act to prevent men from wearing long stockings, knickerbockers and round-about coats when bicycling." The Member for Bruce claimed that if men were allowed to wear long stockings they would next demand the right to wear all sorts of female attire, and finally to be employed in jobs usually done by women. Another member enquired whether the government might allow men to undertake "lighter employments, such as medicine, law, dress-making and millinery which by their very nature belong exclusively to women."[16] Then they debated a bill to enfranchise men on the same terms as women, but the Minister of Education felt that this was "unscriptured" and the bill was defeated.[17] Emily thoroughly enjoyed the Mock Parliament, but she was not optimistic that it would change most men's thinking at least for a while. Yet ultimately she would win. She drew encouragement from the examples of Utah and Idaho which granted woman suffrage in 1896.

Emily's single-minded approach to the improvement of women's lot once upset Lady Aberdeen. Her Excellency felt caught between the two extremes among the members of the National Council of Women. Adelaide Hoodless and her crusade for domestic science in the schools was on one side; pressure from the Stowes and the Dominion Women's Enfranchisement Association was on the other. Ishbel wrote Emily warning her of the danger of alienating other factions in the council, to which Emily sent a conciliatory reply. Lady Aberdeen's objections, she confessed, were forceful, especially regarding "the Alarm" voiced by the council that too much recognition was being given to the suffrage movement. "The latter can afford to wait, and must till a larger understanding of their true position in the World's Economy." Emily fully appreciated "the sacrificial spirit" manifested by Ishbel in devoting so much time, means and energy to the largely thankless "cause so great as the Evolution of our Canadian Women." In fact, Lady Aberdeen's cause was a more Christain enterprise combatting forces

> ... now in operation against us. The bringing together into one fold the various bodies of women, representing differing creed and beliefs out of chaotic darkness and confusions, will come by the light of truth and the highest order.[18]

Since the inaugural meeting in Toronto in 1893, the National Council of Women of Canada had met annually, twice in Ottawa, once each in Toronto, Montreal and Halifax. Every year the council grew larger as more local branches were founded.

For some time Ishbel had been developing a proposal that would be opposed by both doctors and trained nurses and which would leave Emily falling between two stools. Ishbel was dismayed at the lack of health care in the remote areas she had visited, which had neither doctors nor competent nurses. She advocated the formation of a corps of women to serve these communities. They would receive less training and be paid less than nurses who attended hospital schools. They would also act as midwives. Both suggestions alarmed doctors and trained nurses alike. Usurpation of the doctors' role in obstetrics by nurses with inferior training was unacceptable to the medical profession. At the same time, nurses from training schools who had fought hard for years for the right to a living wage were appalled that their wages would be undercut by Lady Aberdeen's proposed nursing order.

Emily sympathized with Ishbel's desire for inexpensive health care for people in remote communities or isolated on the frontiers out west. What Lady Aberdeen was suggesting was that women continue to do what they had long done in places where the number of qualified medical practitioners was inadequate. Emily's own mother, and other women like her, had made medicine from herbs and acted as midwives. Yet, as a doctor, Emily knew that obstetrical patients were safer in the hands of qualified men and women. If Lady Aberdeen wanted to found a nursing order, she should advocate the use of hospital-trained nurses and insist that they be paid at the same rate as other nurses. Only then might trained nurses be permitted to act as midwives in those areas where a doctor could not be reached.

Lady Aberdeen compromised. When her scheme for visiting nurses was about to become a reality, she agreed to use graduate nurses who would deliver babies only in an emergency. Fully qualified nurses would cost more, because each was entitled to a salary of about $300 a year. The amount charged to the patient for a home visit was to be only twenty-five cents an hour and would not cover the entire cost of the nurse's salary. A special fund would have to be raised. Ultimately the nursing order would operate as a visiting home service in towns and cities, as well as in the country and in remote frontier areas. After many delays caused by controversy, the organization received its charter in 1898 as the Victorian Order of Nurses.[19] Because of her concern for health care, Emily approved of Lady Aberdeen's accomplishment. When the Aberdeens' tour of duty in Canada ended in 1898, Ishbel had left behind a noble contribution, a nursing order that to this day provides home care.

Meanwhile, Adelaide Hoodless had succeeded in having legislation introduced for the teaching of domestic science courses in the public schools. Hoodless herself, on behalf of the Department of Education, was campaigning for school boards to use the legislation to start such programmes — work Emily could not fault. In February, 1897, at a meeting of the Farmers' Institute Ladies' Night at Stoney Creek, Adelaide recommended the formation of an organisation for rural women. Soon afterwards, women in the Stoney Creek area held the first meeting of the first Women's Institute of which Mrs. Hoodless was the honorary president. Adelaide is best remembered for the worldwide movement which grew from those modest beginnings at Stoney Creek.[20]

By the time the Aberdeens left Canada, Emily Stowe's lameness was interfering with her activities. She had retired entirely from her medical practice, and was spending so much of her time on Stowe Island that she listed Muskoka as her permanent address in the *Ontario Medical Directory* of 1898. She usually went to Florida to avoid the most severe winter months. Another popular spot was Chautauqua, New York, where she could attend stimulating lectures at the still-popular and greatly expanded Institution.[21]

Contact between the Stowes and Lady Aberdeen continued. Ishbel presided over the International Congress of Women that met in London in June, 1899, which Augusta Stowe Gullen attended as a vice-president. She was also chairman of the sub-committee of the National Council of Women of Canada to improve reform institutions. Emily was then an ex-officio vice-president by virtue of her presidency of the Dominion Women's Enfranchisement Association, an affiliate of the council.[22] The list of standing committees shows which issues the council thought the most important — better protection of women and children, pernicious literature, custodial care of feeble-minded women, care for the aged poor, provision of work for the unemployed, finance, literature and home-reading circles, immigration, the press, raising of a loan for Doukhobor women, aid for the Canadian contingent sent to the Transvaal during the Boer War, and a bureau of information.[23]

For Emily personally, the next important event was the birth, the following year on the twenty-fourth of August,1900, of her only grandson, Frank and Mary Stowe's fourth child. They named him Hudson Jennings, the maiden names of his mother and grandmother.

ELEVEN

The Torch is Passed

THE LIFE OF EMILY STOWE, both as a doctor and as a suffragist, was intertwined with the life of her daughter Augusta. This only daughter was very much the offshoot of her mother; her achievements grew out of Emily's, and she would never have gone as far as she did without the ground her mother had broken ahead of her. At the same time, Augusta lived up to her opportunities and was as devoted as her mother to the struggle for equality in education and politics. They shared the same determination. The main difference between the two women lay in personality and experience, rather than objectives. Emily's many rebuffs left her serious and with a popularity, outside her practice, that rested on her intellectual endeavours. While Augusta also gave lectures, she had the greater gift for making people like her, and was the more sociable.

Emily was fortunate to have had such a daughter to follow the path she had worn. Without Augusta, Emily would have been less well-known after her retirement. Dr. Jenny Trout's memory faded a few years after she stopped practising, and interest in her had waned before Carlotta Hacker revived it in her book, *The Indomitable Lady Doctors*, published in 1974. At the same time, Emily deserves the recognition because she was responsible for more positive advances in the field of medicine than Jenny. Dr. Trout's main contribution was the endowment to the medical college for women in Kingston, which closed down after the session of 1893. The Ontario Medical College for Women, with which Emily was involved, fared better, and from its origins grew the Women's College Hospital in Toronto.

Dr. Augusta Stowe Gullen was a rarity, a Canadian who had no need to leave her country before her fellow-citizens would recognize her as successful. She was the darling of the Toronto press. Although she worked with dedication, both as a doctor and as an educator, Augusta's life was easier than that of her mother. Emily once wrote:

My career has been one of much struggle characterized by the usual persecution which attends everyone who pioneers a new movement or steps out of line with established custom.[1]

Emily spent her last years rather quietly. Crippled with the after-effects of the broken hip, she had difficulty getting about. Finally, the journey to Stowe Island was beyond her; she had to settle for the vicarious pleasure of watching the other family members going off to enjoy it while she remained at 463 Spadina Avenue. Howard Stowe married a second time in 1893.[2] His wife was Lesley Ross, who took over her new stepdaughter, little Emily, now seven, and relieved Emily of that responsibility.

Emily did not always accept her limitations gracefully, and at times her two eldest children annoyed her. She drew up a will, leaving everything to Frank, the youngest, and asked R.S. Hudson, Frank's father-in-law, to witness it. Hudson refused, claiming that he was too closely related to be a witness, and the will never became official.

In April, 1903, Augusta attended a conference of suffragists in New Orleans, where Susan Anthony asked after Dr. Stowe. When Augusta returned home, she noticed a change for the worse in her mother. Aware that she had at most a few weeks to live, Emily made Augusta promise that her body would be cremated. Augusta was perturbed at such a radical suggestion, but Emily retorted: "I have never done an act upon earth to pollute it, and I do not wish to do so in dissolution."[3]

The end came on the thirtieth of April, 1903, and the funeral service was held at 463 Spadina Avenue. Two old friends of Emily's officiated, Reverend Dr. Parker and Reverend Sunderland, the latter of the Unitarian Church. Sunderland's presence confirmed Emily's unorthodox philosophy, which was described as "advanced" in a newspaper account of the funeral. The service was brief and informal, followed by "O Rest in the Lord" sung by Mrs. Palmer, an "intimate friend of the deceased." The house was filled with "floral tributes." The obituary that appeared in the *Canadian Journal of Medicine and Surgery* noted the appropriateness of the scripture: "Though I speak with the tongues of men and of angels, and have not charity, I am become as sounding brass, or a tinkling cymbal." "And now abideth faith, hope, charity, but the greatest of these is charity." (1 Cor. xiii)[4]

Augusta overcame her distaste and carried out her mother's wish. Because the nearest crematorium in Canada was in far-off Montreal, the body was taken to Buffalo, New York. For some years Emily's ashes reposed in the basement of 463 Spadina Avenue. Eventually they disappeared, and no one seems to know where they went.

Emily died intestate, so that her estate had to be divided evenly among her three children. Augusta was determined to have Howard's share of Stowe Island, but she did not have enough money to purchase it from the estate. She caused some ill feeling when she forced the sale of the Church Street house so that she could use her share of the proceeds to buy out her brother's interest in the island.[5]

On the twenty-fifth of May, after she had learned of Emily's death, and to express her sympathy, Susan Anthony wrote to Augusta from the National American Woman Suffrage Association headquarters, situated at 17 Madison Street, Rochester, New York. Miss Anthony's name was on the letterhead as the honorary president of the association. She recalled meeting Dr. Stowe while she was at Dr. Lozier's school in New York in 1867.

> Your mother was a pioneer in every sense of the word, and I liked her for her very self. I little thought when I saw you at New Orleans that you would be called to bear this sorrow so soon, but we all have to go sooner or later, and with myself, working hard to get Vol. IV located among its fellows. I send you by same mail a copy of the book.[6]

The volume four she mentioned was the last one in her work, *The History of Woman Suffrage.* Miss Anthony lived another three years, dying in 1906 at age eighty-six.

Emily had made scant progress during her life towards the enfranchisement of women, although her groundwork was impressive.
Her successes as a doctor were more apparent; she was unique as the
first woman medical practitioner (not counting Dr. James Barry), and
she sat on the committee that that founded the Ontario Medical College for Women, the forerunner of the Women's College Hospital. She
ran her substantial practice along the conservative homeopathic lines
with a large measure of common sense, and with the sympathy that
endeared her to her patients. She did not live long enough to see the
closing of the Ontario Medical College for Women. The last session of
the college was in 1905, after which women were admitted to the
Faculty of Medicine at the University of Toronto on the same terms as
men. Emily would not have mourned the closing of the school; it was
a stopgap measure until the university would consent to coeducation
in the medical faculty. By 1903, the year of Emily's death, the Trinity
Medical College was absorbed into the university medical faculty.

The Ontario Medical College for Women had served its purpose.
By the time it, too, was absorbed by the University of Toronto, the staff
numbered thirty-two, ten of whom were women.[7] Augusta, who had
started as a demonstrator in anatomy in 1883, was a professor when it
closed, and since 1899 she had been a consulting physician at the Toronto Western Hospital.

After moving from Euclid Avenue to rented premises on Manning
Avenue, the Toronto Western Hospital purchased the site at 399
Bathurst Street in 1899. Important benefactors were two brothers,
David and Alexander Fasken, both successful lawyers and business-
men who had been born of Scottish parents near Elora, Ontario, and
who had made the arrangements for the purchase of the property.
Their sister was the wife of one of the founding doctors, John Fer-
guson. On the site a large farm house served as the maternity wing.
When more space was required another founding doctor, George
Carveth, suggested the erection of a large tent. Used in summer and
winter, it was heated by steam coils between its canvas walls when
necessary. In summer other tents often stood nearby until the hospital
could afford a permanent building. On the first of November, 1896,
Augusta delivered the first baby at the new hospital. The child was a

boy, and at the time the Western was hardly more than the original dispensary.[8]

In 1905 the Tory government of Premier George William Ross was out of power. The Dominion Women's Enfranchisement Association and the Women's Christian Temperance Union decided to lead another deputation to the Ontario Legislature. Perhaps the new Liberal premier, James Pliny Whitney, would be more open-minded than his predecessors. This time, the women's champion among the members of the House was John Smith, Liberal member for Peel. John Waters, their previous advocate, had retired twelve years before. To Augusta Stowe Gullen's chagrin the new premier was evasive. When, on the eleventh of May, John Smith moved a second reading of his bill to give all women the provincial franchise, the debate that followed was "intensely silly."[9] Amidst laughter and clapping, Smith withdrew his bill.

He tried again in 1906, but this time the motion for a second reading was defeated by ninety-nine votes to six. As a counterweight, a large meeting in Toronto on the twentieth of November, over which the mayor, Emerson Coatsworth, presided, passed a resolution in favour of extending both the provincial and federal franchise to women.[10] The next year, 1907, Augusta, as president of the Dominion Women's Enfranchisement Association, with her executive, resolved on a pithier name for the organization, in the hope that it would have more appeal. They chose Canadian Suffrage Association. Augusta remained its president until 1911.

When John Smith tried yet again in 1908 to introduce his bill, Premier Whitney urged the members to protect "the dignity of the House and the dignity of the women of this country." Allan Studholme, a Labour member from East Hamilton, sided with Smith. Studholme was to be a fighter for women's rights for the next ten years. During the period 1905 to 1909, one of Premier Whitney's favourite arguments was that God had placed women where they were, that "woman's place was assigned by a Great Power."[11] The support of a man like Studholme, who was far to the left, must have been a source of irritation to either old-line party and, unfortunately, probably did the women's cause at least as much harm as good. [12]

The suffragists were particularly active in 1909. In March the largest deputation yet went to the Ontario Legislature. Dr. Augusta Stowe Gullen presented a petition to the House with 100,000 signatures on it. Nevertheless, Premier Whitney remained unmoved, and when Studholme presented his bill it was defeated.[13] The Congress of the International Council of Women met at the University of Toronto from the twenty-fourth to the thirtieth of June. Lady Aberdeen, still the president, sent greetings but was unable to attend, since Lord Aberdeen was now Viceroy of Ireland and, as his consort, Ishbel was fully occupied with her duties in Dublin Castle. Beforehand, the committee of the National Council of Women of Canada and the various subcomittees of local councils had prepared a brochure entitled "Who's Who at the Congress." Suffragists from all over North America and Europe attended. Among them was Mrs. Adam Shortt, the former Elizabeth Smith who had corresponded with Augusta in 1879 concerning medical training at Kingston, and who, in 1884, was among the first medical graduates from Queen's. This vast gathering, and the many reports about it, gave impetus to the cause of women; the following year the National Council of Women of Canada took the step Emily had long advocated by endorsing woman suffrage.

In November, 1909, the best-known British suffragette, Emmeline Pankhurst, came to speak in Toronto. Augusta gave a tea for the visitor at 461 Spadina Avenue. Her nephew, Hudson Stowe, growing up at number 463, was invited to come next door to meet Mrs. Pankhurst. She was but one of the best known suffragists Hudson recalled meeting at his aunt's house. When Augusta entertained them she hired Coles as the caterers, and a delighted small boy was welcome to enjoy the confections. Reporter Jean Graham gave an account of Mrs. Pankhurst's visit in an unidentified newspaper which Augusta kept. The meeting was at Massey Hall on the twentieth and, according to Graham, Mrs. Pankhurst was a born orator; Graham admired her "conquest of many men listeners."[14]

The following year women were enfranchised in the State of Washington, while Dr. Augusta Stowe Gullen was appointed to the senate of the University of Toronto to represent the medical profession.[15] Emily would have been thrilled at the progress of women in the field of medicine. Now they were able to study alongside men in sev-

eral universities, and the honour to Augusta was a tribute to her ca-
pabilities as a doctor. The appointment was another Stowe first;
Augusta was the first woman doctor to hold a post of significant authority. No other woman seems to have been involved in the early
medical associations in the city: the Toronto Medical Society, Toronto
Pathological Society, the Toronto Clinical Society, or the Ontario
Medical Library — all of which were started in the second half of the
nineteenth century.[16]

Augusta led a much easier life than Emily. Since the Gullens had
no children Augusta was able to concentrate more on her practice and
on her work for the Canadian Suffrage Association and the National
Council of Women of Canada. Unlike Emily, Augusta lived to see the
fruits of their toil. Sympathy for woman suffrage was growing, yet the
legislators remained unmoved. At the federal level, Prime Minister
Robert Borden admitted in 1912 that if the provinces would enfranchise women, the government in Ottawa could then act. In 1914, Toronto City Council, in response to a request from the Canadian Suffrage Association, held a referendum to ascertain the views of the
public. In all, thirty-three referendums were held between 1914 and
1916, and all were favourable to the cause.[17]

Emily Stowe's family remembered her with fondness. Many were
the stories of Grandma Stowe that Augusta, Howard and Frank told
the grandchildren, who now numbered six — Frank's Marie, Hilda
and Hudson; Howard's Emily, and his daughters by his second wife,
Lesley Ross (born in 1903 after Emily's death), and Bernice Cornelia
(born in 1905).

Family friends and Emily's colleagues also cherished her memory.
On the twenty-fifth of June, 1910, Mr. and Mrs. Charles Edward
Peabody held a lawn fête at their home, 21 Rosedale Road, to raise
money for a bronze bust to be sculpted by Walter S. Allward. The
price of admission was twenty-five cents.[18] The bust was presented to
Toronto City Hall, at a ceremony on the thirty-first of October, 1913. It
was unveiled by two of Emily's grandchildren, Hudson, Frank's son,
then thirteen, and Lesley, Howard's daughter, aged ten.

In 1914, not to be put off by preparation and participation in war,
a deputation appeared before the new Conservative premier, William

Hearst, to ask that the municipal vote be extended to married women of property. Like his predecessors, he stalled that year and again in 1916.

Nevertheless, Augusta was feeling more optimistic than at any time in the past. The tide was turning; the Ontario politicians would not be able to hold out much longer. In 1916 Manitoba, Saskatchewan, Alberta and British Columbia had all granted provincial and municipal suffrage to women who met the same qualifications as men. In Ontario, franchise groups and the Women's Christian Temperance Union prepared an enormous petition from all over the province demanding full suffrage. Then, in 1917, the Liberal opposition included woman suffrage in its platform, and in February, in the course of a debate on a private member's bill for woman suffrage, Hearst's Conservatives, out of the blue, changed tactics and supported the bill. Royal assent came on the twelfth of April, and all women voters who qualified were eligible to vote at both municipal and provincial elections.[19] All that remained to be won was the federal vote. This was granted to female relatives of members of the armed forces on the twentieth of September, 1917, and to all women on the twenty-fourth of May 1918.

In Ontario the battle had been won, and Augusta could be proud of her role and of her mother's in achieving enfranchisement. Of the other provinces, Nova Scotia succumbed on the twenty-sixth of April, 1918; New Brunswick on the seventeenth of April, 1919; Prince Edward Island on the third of May, 1922; but Quebec did not yield until the twenty-fifth of April, 1940. (Newfoundland legislated the enfranchisement of women on the thirteenth of April, 1925, before it joined the Canadian confederation.)[20]

In the four western provinces the right to hold office came at the same time as enfranchisement. Ontario delayed two years, until the twenty-fourth of April, 1919. New Brunswick took five years, until the ninth of March, 1924. Augusta Stowe Gullen, who lived until September, 1943, was able to rejoice over each of these changes, and especially over the famous judicial decision of 1929, fostered by Emily Murphy, that women were "persons" under the British North America Act.

Augusta wrote two pamphlets. The first, published in 1906, was a "Brief History of the Ontario Medical College for Women." The second, in 1932, was the "History of the Formation of the National Council of Women of Canada." She based this on the proceedings of the congress in Washington in 1888, which her mother had attended, and that in Chicago in 1903, when Lady Aberdeen agreed to preside over the International Council. Lady Aberdeen's presidency of the National Council of Women of Canada, Augusta wrote, had acted like a magnet, drawing in many women and organizations that might otherwise have remained aloof.[21] Augusta sent six copies of her second pamphlet to Lady Aberdeen. Ishbel was living in the Aberdeens' retirement home, Cromar, near the village of Tarland, on the Deeside not far from Balmoral, the Royal Family's autumn holiday residence. On the eighteenth of July, 1932, writing from Cromar, Ishbel thanked Dr. Stowe Gullen for the gift, which she would treasure.[22]

Among Augusta's many papers, now in the libraries of Victoria and Wilfrid Laurier universities, is the account of a Jubilee year of women's equality — described as a fiftieth anniversary of the first international union of women for self defence. The year chosen was 1932, which suggested that women were commemorating an event of 1882. Among the landmarks cited was the Ontario Medical College for Women that had opened its doors in October 1883. Perhaps it qualified because in 1882 the college was in its planning stage.

The final tribute Augusta Stowe Gullen received was the Jubilee Medal of 1935, commemorating the twenty-fifth anniversary of the accession of King George V to the throne.[23] Whatever honour came to Augusta was a tribute, in part, to her mother, in whose footsteps she so faithfully followed.

While modern feminists might disparage Adelaide Hoodless as a reactionary, without taking into account the Victorian world where her views were considered advanced, they have less cause to ridicule Emily Stowe. Her intense belief in equality, in the right of women to enjoy the same education as men, and in woman suffrage are more in tune with the contemporary mood. At the same time, her "woman's sphere" theme is anathema to those feminists who seek to break down all barriers in the home, the workplace, the church and sports.

The barriers are not yet all down, but Emily would be astonished, although not shocked, at a woman warden in a prison for men, women ordained for the ministry, girls serving as altar attendants, women driving bulldozers and buses, girls playing ice hockey on teams intended for boys, women Mounties and police on municipal forces, or women cadets at Royal Military Colleges. To Emily these roles lay within man's sphere. Medicine and politics, however, were not man's preserve; they belonged to both sexes. The appointment, in 1988, of a woman doctor as Medical Officer of Health for the sprawling Regional Municipality of York that lies north of Metropolitan Toronto would have been entirely appropriate in Emily's eyes.

If Emily Stowe could look in on the world of the 1990s, she would be disappointed that, having acquired the right to hold office, so few women have sought and won seats in the provincial legislature and the federal Parliament. She would be more satisfied with women's successes in municipal politics and would rejoice also at their invasion into the practice not only of medicine but of law, the traditional school for politicians. In the last decade of the twentieth century approximately half the students that attend university classes in medicine and law are women.

In March, 1981, the country remembered Emily Stowe on the occasion of her 150th anniversary of her birth. The Post Office issued a seventeen-cent commemorative stamp, the standard rate for a letter at the time. Ceremonies to celebrate the birthday took place in Ottawa and in Norwich. Today two plaques stand as lasting memorials to Emily. One plaque is in the village of Norwich, where she lived for several years; the other plaque is closer to her birthplace, in the Summerville Cemetery on the east side of local road fifty-nine and south of the ninth concession of Norwich Township.

ENDNOTES

Abbreviations

AMT   Academy of Medicine, Toronto

DAB   *Dictionary of American Biography*, American Council of Learned Societies, various editors. (New York: Scribner's, 1927 onwards).

DCB   *Dictionary of Canadian Biography*, various editors. (Toronto: University of Toronto Press, 1966 onwards).

DNB   *Dictionary of National Biography*, Sir Leslie Stephen and Sir Sidney Lee, editors. (Oxford: University Press, 1917 onwards).

HJSG   Family genealogy supplied by Emily's grandson, Hudson Jennings Stowe.

MTL   Metropolitan Toronto Library

NDA   Norwich District Archives

NDHS   Norwich and District Historical Society

OA   Ontario Archives

VUL ASG   Victoria University Library, Augusta Stowe Gullen collection, on microfilm or in boxes.

Chapter 1: Equal Among Friends

1. Carlotta Hacker, *The Indomitable Lady Doctors* (Toronto: Clarke Irwin, 1974), pp. 3-16, chapter on Dr. Barry based on Isobel Rae, *The Strange Story of Dr. James Barry*. (London: Longmans, 1958).

2. HJSG

3. DAB, vol. 6, pp. 421-422; David Brearley, *Hotbed of Treason: Norwich and the Rebellion of 1837* (Archives Committee, NDHS 1988, Norwich, Ontario, NOJ 1P0), p. 15.

4. MTL, Baldwin Room, Peter Lossing Papers. Letters, 24 Oct., 1810; 17 Feb., 1811; Sodom, p. 190.

5. Ibid., letter 25, Feb. 1811.

6. Ibid., letter 18, Mar. 1815.

7. NDHS, *South of Sodom: the History of South Norwich* (NDHS: May 1983), p. 22, Peter Lossing's Map 1820; MTL, Baldwin Room, Peter Lossing Papers. Marriage certificate of George Southwick and Paulina Howard.

8. Ibid., letter from Providence Seminary, 12 June 1827.

9. Emily P. Weaver, "Pioneer Canadian Women," *Canadian Magazine*, 17 Feb. n. yr., p. 314. Copy in Emily Stowe envelope at AMT; HJSG.

10. *South of Sodom*, p. 190.

11. HJSG.

12. Joanne Thompson, "The Influence of Dr. Emily Howard Stowe on the Woman Suffrage Movement in Canada." *Ontario History*, vol. 54, (December 1962): 259.

13. Janet Ray, *Emily Stowe* (Don Mills, Ontario: Fitzhenry and Whiteside Canadians Series), 1968, p. 5.

14. *South of Sodom*, pp, 21,130, 132.

15. Edwin Seaborn, *The March of Medicine in Western Ontario*. (London, University of Western Ontario: Ryerson, 1944), pp. 262-263; DCB, vol. 9, biog. of John Rolph.

16. William L. Smith, *The Pioneers of Old Ontario*. (Makers of Canada Series, Toronto: Oxford University Press, 1923), pp. 13-18, George N. Morang's article.

17. James Harvey Young, *The Toadstool Millionaires: A Social History: Patent Medicine before Federal Regulation*. (Princeton, N. J.: Princeton University Press), 1961, p. 44.

18. William Renwick Riddell, "Popular Medicine in Upper Canada a Century Ago." Ontario Historical Society *Papers and Records*, vol. 25 (1929), p. 398.

19. Ibid., p. 402.

20. Young, *Toadstool*, pp. 68-69.

21. William Canniff, *The Medical Profession in Upper Canada 1783-1850*. (Toronto: William Briggs, 1894) p. 305.

22. *South of Sodom*, p. 300.

23. Brearley, *Hotbed*, pp. 11-14.

Chapter 2: Regina versus Lossing

1. Brearley, *Hotbed*, p. 12.

2. Ibid., p. 118.

3. Colin Read and Ronald J. Stagg, *The Rebellion of 1837 in Upper Canada*. (Toronto: Champlain Society, 1985), pp. 203-204, John Treffry, Summerville, Norwich, 24 June 1838 to his brother George Treffry in Exeter, England.

4. Brearley, *Hotbed*, pp 20 and 96 note 23.

5. Colin Read, *The Rising in Western Upper Canada 1837-8; The Duncombe Revolt and After*. (Toronto: University of Toronto Press, 1982), p. 102; Brearley, *Hotbed*, pp. 22-24.

6. *South of Sodom*, p. 107.

7. Brearley, *Hotbed*, p. 27.

8. Seaborn, *Medicine in Western Ontario*, p. 194; Read, *Rising*, p. 143, 226; Read and Stagg, *Rebellion*, p. 237, note 151; MTL, Baldwin Room, Peter Lossing Papers, marriage certificate, 13 Dec. 1815. Joseph Lancaster Senior and his wife Hannah were among the witnesses.

9. Brearley, *Hotbed*, p. 43.

10. Ibid., pp. 43-44.

11. Ibid., p. 52.

12. Ibid., p. 92; Amelia Poldon, *The Amelia Poldon History of the Norwiches*. (NDHS: Norwich, 1985), p. 33.

13. Read and Stagg, *Rebellion*, p. 329.

14. Brearley, *Hotbed*, p. 86.

15. Mary Beacock Fryer, *Volunteers and Redcoats; Rebels and Raiders: A Military History of the Rebellions in Upper Canada*. (Toronto: Dundurn Press, 1987), p. 119; Brearley, *Hotbed*, Foreword, p. III.

16. Ibid., pp 32, 35.

17. Ibid., p. 76.

Chapter 3: First Woman Principal

1. *South of Sodom*, p. 149.

2. Ibid., p. 118.

3. Brock and Oxford school records, NDHS, 1848-1850; OA, Annual Reports of School Superintendents, North and South Norwich Townships. The original Township of Norwich was divided in 1855. The two townships remained separate until 1975 when they were again united.

4. Arthur G. Dorland, *Former Days and Quaker Ways*. (Picton: *Gazette* Publishing Co. Ltd., 1965). Chapter 10 gives the background. West Lake operated from 1841 until 1865, and was the forerunner of Pickering College, which reopened in 1878 in Pickering Township.

5. Alison Prentice, *The School Promoters*. (Toronto: McClelland and Stewart, 1982), p. 18.

6. William J. Karr, *The Training of Teachers in Ontario*. PhD thesis, Queen's, 1916. (Ottawa: R.J. Taylor, Printer,1916), p. 15.

7. Edwin C. Guillet, *The Cause of Education*. (Toronto: University of Toronto Press, 1960), pp. 153, 264-265.

8. *Proceedings of the ceremony laying the chief cornerstone of the Normal and Model Schools*, Ontario Institute for Studies in Education Library, Toronto, map at end of book.

9. Karr, *Training*, p. 17.

10. Douglas F. Reville, *History of the County of Brant*. 2 vols. (Brantford: Hurley Printing Co. Ltd., 1920), vol. 1, p. 227.

11. *Dictionary of Hamilton Biography*, vol. 1, T. Melville Bailey ed. (Hamilton: W.L. Griffin Ltd., 1981), biog. of Ormiston, p. 161; VUL ASG, box 5 on microfilm, numbered 9, Brown Album.

12. NDA, copy of a form Emily filled out for Henry J. Morgan to include in his book *Canadian Men and Women of the Time* in 1898. She wrote that she was married in Norwichville but gave no other details.

13. Ray, *Emily Stowe*, p. 13.

14. Robert Clark and Others. *A Glimpse of the Past: Centennial History of Brantford and Brant County*. (Brantford: Brantford Historical Society, 1966), p. 14; OA, Census of 1851, Reel 947, p. 65, line 12, Stowe, John, Tailor; Census of 1861, Reel 1008, p. 111, line 12, Stowe, John, Carriage Maker, wife Emily, line 22, John Stowe, Tailor; 1871 Census, Reel 611, Division 3, p. 58, line 10, Stowe, John, Gentleman.

15. Dorland, *Former Days*, p. 114.

16. AMT, Augusta Stowe envelope, incomplete clipping, undated; also Charles Godfrey, *Medicine for Ontario: A History*. (Belleville: Mika, 1979), p. 289.

17. *Tweedsmuir History of Mount Pleasant, Brant County*. Microfilm of a scrapbook compiled by the Women's Institute. OA, MS8, Reel 1, pages are unpaginated, long note on the Stowes.

18. Godfrey, *Medicine*, p. 157.

19. Ibid., p. 192.

20. Ibid., p. 279; Read and Stagg, *Rebellion*, pp. 237-238.

21. C.D. Haggensen and E.B. Wyndham, *One Hundred Years of Medicine*. (New York: Sheridan House, 1943), p. 9.

22. Ruth J. Abram ed. *Send Us a Lady Physician: Women Doctors in America 1835-1920*. (New York: W.W. Morton & Co., 1985), pp. 47-48.

23. Godfrey, *Medicine*. 176-177.

24. Ibid., pp. 193-194.

25. DAB, biog. of Dr. Trudeau, vol. 10, p. 4.

26. Weaver, "Pioneer", p. 315.

27. R.Y. Keers, *Pulmonary Tuberculosis: A Journey Down the Centuries* (London: Baillière Tindall, 1978), pp. 68-70.

28. Tweedsmuir History, under schools; Ray, Emily Stowe, pp. 14-15.

29. Nuffield Provincial Hospitals Trust, *Medical History and Medical Care: A Symposium of Perspectives*. (London: Oxford University Press, 1971, John Brotherston, "Evolution of Medical Practice," pp. 88-89.

30. HJSG.

31. Stanley Brice Frost, *McGill University*. (Montreal: McGill-Queen's Press, 1980), pp. 141-144.

32. Godfrey, *Medicine*, p. 186. Godfrey states that on this occasion Emily applied again to Victoria, which is incorrect; she had been turned down by Victoria before she went to Normal School, and did not apply again.

33. Thompson, "Influence", p. 254, also note 12.

34. Regina Markell Morantz-Sanches, *Sympathy and Science: Women Physicians in American Medicine*. (New York: Oxford University Press, 1985), p. 75.

Chapter 4: Medical Student

1. Hacker, *Indomitable*, p. 235, note 7.

2. DAB, vol. 6, p. 480, biog. of Clemence Sophia Lozier.

3. Esther Pohl Lovejoy, *Women Doctors of the World*. (New York: Macmillan, 1957), p. 111.

4. Catherine Lyle Cleverdon, *The Woman Suffrage Movement in Canada*. (Toronto: University of Toronto Press, 1974), p. 22.

5. Ezra Hurlburt Stafford, M.B., *Medicine, Surgery and Hygiene in the Century*. (London, Toronto, Philadelphia: Lincott Publishing Co., 1901), p. 49.

6. Ibid., chapter 18 is a summary of these anesthetics; also p. 406; DNB, biography of Sir James Simpson.

7. Young, *Toadstool*, p. 172.

8. Ibid., p. 68.

9. David M. Ellis, James A. Frost, Harold C. Syrett, Harry J. Carmen, *A History of New York State*. (Ithaca, N.Y.: New York State Historical Association, Cornell University Press, 1967), p. 461.

10. John A. Kouwenhoven, *The Columbia Historical Portrait of New York*. (New York: Doubleday, 1953), p. 265.

11. Ellis, Frost, Syrett, Carmen, *History*, p. 297.

12. VUL ASG, box 3, folder F, copy of the front page, *New York Times*, undated, but with many letters from 1864 and 1865 written while need for the hospital was under discussion.

13. James Joseph Walsh, *History of Medicine in New York*. 5 vols. (New York: Americana Society Inc., 1919), vol. 2, p. 555.

14. Ibid., pp. 553, 555.

15. Morantz-Sanches, *Sympathy*, pp. 47-49.

16. Ibid., p. 73.

17. John Murray Gibbon and Mary S. Mathewson, R.N. B.S., *Three Centuries of Canadian Nursing*. (Toronto: Macmillan, 1927), pp. 111-112.

18. Walsh, *History*, p. 555.

19. Morantz-Sanchez, *Sympathy*, pp. 74-75.

20. Ibid., pp. 211, 225-226.

21. H. Strange, M.D., *Medical Directory for the Province of Ontario 1898*. (Hamilton: C.E. Steward, Publisher, 1898). The reference to Dr. Stowe reads, "Stowe, Emily Howard, Muskoka, Member of College of Physicians and Surgeons of Ontario 1880; in practice prior to 1st January 1850. M.D. New York Medical College for Women, 1867."

22. VUL, ASG, box 5, microfilm, report of the 4th annual commencement, New York Medical College for Women, incorrectly hand-dated 1870 or 1871.

23. Weaver, "Pioneer", p. 315.

24. H. Strange, .M.D. *A Medical Directory for the Province of Ontario 1869*. (Hamilton: C.E. Steward, Publisher, 1869), p. 47, "List of Homeopathic Members of the College of Physicians and Surgeons of Ontario" includes Joseph J. Lancaster, M.D., London, Middlesex.

25. Seaborn, *March*, pp. 190, 194, 197.

26. Ibid., p. 199.

27. Toronto *Globe*, issues for 11 Nov. and 3 Dec., 1867.

28. *Toronto Directory 1868-1869*, p. 345. The directories are in the Metropolitan Toronto Library.

29. Strange, *Medical Directory 1869*, pp. 45-47.

30. Ibid., p. 52.

31. Godfrey, *Medicine*, pp. 186, 223.

32. *Toronto Directory 1870*.

33. George W. Spragge, "The Trinity Medical College." *Ontario History*, vol. 68 #2, June 1966, pp. 72, 75.

34. Stafford, *Medicine*, p. 403.

35. Morantz-Sanchez, *Sympathy*, p. 189.

Chapter 5: Dr. Stowe versus Dr. Trout

1. Hacker, *Indomitable*, pp. 41, 42.

2. Ibid., p. 20.

3. Ibid., p. 42.

4. D.W. Gullett, *A History of Dentistry in Canada*. (Toronto: University of Toronto Press, 1960) pp. 22, 43, 49-50, 58-62.

5. Ibid., pp. 61, 62.

6. Records of the Royal College of Dental Surgeons, Toronto.

7. Hacker, *Indomitable*, pp. 41, 42.

8. OA, MU7320, envelope on Ella Jennings.

9. HJSG.

10. Ibid.

11. VUL ASG, box 3, folders E-F,G.

12. Thompson, "Influence", p. 256, note 22.

13. Henry J. Morgan, *Canadian Men and Women of the Time*. (Toronto: Briggs, 1898), pp. 973-974.

14. Wendy Mitchinson and Janice Dickin McGinnis, eds., *Essays in the History of Canadian Medicine*. (Toronto: McClelland and Stewart 1988), Heather MacDougall, "Public Health and the 'Sanitary Idea' in Toronto 1866-1890", p. 62.

15. Ibid., pp. 64-71.

16. Hacker, *Indomitable*, p. 46.

17. A. Adams, M.D., *Electricity: its Mode of Action Upon the Human Frame and Diseases in which it is beneficial*. (Toronto: 58 Bay St., n. yr.) unpaginated.

18. Hacker, *Indomitable*, pp. 46-47.

19. Godfrey, *Medicine*, p. 200.

20. Young, *Toadstool*, p. 172.

21. Godfrey, *Medicine*, p. 200.

22. Ray, *Emily Stowe*, p. 52.

23. Charles Bruce Sissons, *A History of Victoria University*. (Toronto: University of Toronto Press, 1952), p. 142.

24. Godfrey, *Medicine*, p. 60.

25. Spragge, "Trinity", pp. 76-77.

26. Ibid., p. 81.

27. Ibid., pp. 84-85.

Chapter 6: Licensed at Last

1. W. Stewart Wallace, *History of the University of Toronto*. (Toronto: University of Toronto Press, 1927), p. 105.

2. AMT, Aikins Papers, first envelope, unnumbered, anonymous typescript, probably by Norman B. Gwyn, quoting an article by F.N.G. Starr, *University Monthly*, 1902, pp. 3,4.

3. Hacker, *Indomitable*, p. 56.

4. Thompson, "Influence", p. 257, from VUL, ASG, scrapbook 3, I,K.

5. Ray, *Emily Stowe*, p. 27.

6. VUL ASG, box 5 on microfilm, from Wilfred Laurier University collection, newspaper clipping, n.d.

7. HJSG.

8. VUL ASG, box 5 on microfilm, newspaper clipping, n.d.

9. Godfrey, *Medicine*, p. 179.

10. Heather MacDougall, "Public Health in Toronto's Municipal Politics: the Canniff Years 1883-1890." *Bulletin of the History of Medicine.* #55, 1981, pp. 186, 187.

11. MacDougall, "Sanitary Idea", p. 79.

12. Ibid., p. 80.

13. Mary Adelaide Nutting and Lavinia L. Dock, R.N., *History of Nursing*. 4 vols. (New York and London: G.F. Putnam's Sons, 1907-1935), vol. 4 (1912), p. 131.

14. VUL ASG, box 5, microfilm, newspaper article, May 1889.

15. Nutting and Dock, *History*, p. 131.

16. Hacker, *Indomitable*, p. 56, from diary of Elizabeth Smith, 23 Apr. 1879, Adam Shortt papers, Queen's University Archives. Miss Smith married the famous political economist.

17. Ibid., p. 57, from Adam Shortt papers.

18. VUL. ASG, box 3, folder A, certificate.

19. Ibid., box 1, microfilm, report on Victoria Convocation, newspaper clipping 1 Aug. 1883.

20. Jesse Edgar Middleton, *The Municipality of Toronto: A History*. 3 vols.

(Toronto: The Dominion Publishing Co., 1923), vol. 3, p. 253, biog. of Frederick Cecil Gullen, John's nephew.

21. Gullett, *Dentistry*, p. 43.

23. *Tweedsmuir History*, section on the Stowe family, unpaginated.

24. Hacker, *Indomitable*, p. 21, newspaper clipping from scrapbook #4, Wilfred Laurier University.

25. AMT *The Medical Register 1898*.

26. VUL ASG, box 3, folder H, letter by Ms. Hacker.

27. Hacker, *Indomitable*, p. 58

Chapter 7: Another Stowe First (1881-1883)

1. Wadsworth, Unwin and Brown, *Historical Atlas of Oxford County O n - tario.* (Toronto: Walker and Miles, 1876), p.ix.

2. Thompson, "Influence," p. 256.

3. Cleverdon, *Suffrage*, pp. 20-21.

4. MacDougall, "Sanitary Idea," p. 79.

5. Ibid., p. 80.

6. *Tweedsmuir History*, OA, MS 8, Reel 1, on the Stowe family, this part unpaginated.

7. Cleverdon, *Suffrage*, p. 21.

8. VUL ASG, box 5, microfilm, clipping on the lecture at the town hall, Brantford.

9. *Bystander*, Apr. 1883, quoted in Wallace, *History*, p. 103.

10. VUL ASG, box 5, microfilm, newspaper clippings, undated.

11. Hacker, *Indomitable*, p. 47.

12. DCB, vol. 11, pp. 53-54, biog. of Michael Barrett.

13. VUL, ASG, box 5, microfilm, clipping, 9 Mar. 1883. It referred incorrectly to the "Canadian Women's Suffrage Association.

14. Gibbon and Mathewson, *Three Centuries*, p. 186.

15. Heather MacDougall, "Public Health," pp. 198, 200.

16. Ibid., pp. 189, 192.

17. VUL, ASG, box 3, folder A, contains the certificates.

Chapter 8: Stowe versus Trout — Two Medical Colleges

1. VUL, ASG, box 1, microfilm, clipping dated 1 Aug. 1883 on the convocation, also an article on Augusta's wedding.

2. Hacker, *Indomitable*, pp. 47-49.

3. Women's College Hospital, "History of the Women's College Hospital." Mimeographed typescript, MTL, p. 1.

4. VUL, ASG, box 3, folder C, deed to Stowe Island.

5. Ibid., folder A, *Globe*, Sat. 17 June 1895.

6. Augusta Stowe-Gullen, "A Brief History of the Ontario Medical College for Women," pamphlet, 1906, OA, pp. 4-6.

7. Hacker, *Indomitable*, pp. 49-50; Hilda Neatby, *Queen's University 1841-1917*. 2 vols. (Montreal: Queen's-McGill Press, vol. 1, 1978), vol. 1, pp. 213-216.

8. Ibid., p. 217.

9. Hacker, *Indomitable*, pp. 51-52.

10. HJSG.

11. Wallace, *History*, pp. 105-106.

12. MacDougall, "Sanitary Idea," pp. 82-83.

13. Cleverdon, *Suffrage*, p. 23.

14. VUL, ASG, box 5, microfilm, short biography of John Stowe Sr.

15. Gibbon and Mathewson, *Three Centuries*, p. 186.

16. MacDougall, "Sanitary Idea", p. 84; Middleton, *Toronto*, vol. 1, p. 328.

17. Gibbon and Mathewson, *Three Centuries*, p. 112.

18. Spragge, "Trinity Medical College", p. 87; Sissons, *Victoria*, p. 190.

19. OA, MU 7320, Hannah H. Jennings envelope.

20. Ibid., Ella A Jennings envelope.

21. Rosa L. Shaw, *Proud Heritage: a History of the National Council of Women of Canada*. (Toronto: Ryerson, 1957), p. 2.

Chapter 9: Death of John Stowe

1. DAB, vol. 11, pp. 35-36, biog. of Anna Howard Shaw.

2. Thompson, "Influence", pp. 259-260.

3. Cleverdon, *Suffrage*, p. 24.

4. VUL. ASG, box 5, microfilm, newspaper clipping dated ? May 1889.

7. Ibid., report on Dr. Stowe's return from Chicago.

8. Thompson, "Influence," p. 261.

9. VUL, ASG, box 1, microfilm, last item.

10. OA, MU 7320, Emily Stowe envelope.

11. VUL, ASG, box 5, microfilm, clipping with headline, n.d.

12. Thompson, "Influence," p. 262, from unidentified newspaper clipping dated Fri. 13 June 1890.

13. Cheryl MacDonald, *Adelaide Hoodless; Domestic Crusader*. (Toronto: Dundurn, 1986), p. 13.

14. VUL. ASG, box 5, microfilm, report on the convention, undated.

15. Thompson, "Influence," p. 262.

16. Women's College Hospital, "History," pp.1-2.

17. Middleton, *Toronto*, vol. 2, p. 776.

18. VUL ASG, box 3, folder A, *Globe* article 17 Aug. 1895.

19. HJSG.

20. VUL ASG, box 1, microfilm, n.d.

21. Ibid., report of the school board meeting, numbered 35.

22. HJSG.

23. OA, MU 7320, Emily Stowe envelope.

24. VUL ASG, box 3, folder D, report of the convention.

Chapter 10: Emily and Ishbel, 1893-1896

1. VUL ASG, box 3, folder D; MacDonald, *Hoodless*, pp. 27-28.

2. Ibid., pp. 27-28.

3. Doris French, *Ishbel and the Empire: A Biography of Lady Aberdeen*. (Toronto: Dundurn, 1988), pp. 127, 152.

4. Information supplied by Hudson Stowe.

5. MacDonald, *Hoodless*, p. 30.

6. French, *Ishbel*, p. 153.

7. Cleverdon, *Suffrage*, p. 26-27.

8. French, *Ishbel*, p. 51.

9. MacDonald, *Hoodless*, pp. 50-51.

10. VUL ASG, box 4, report on the visit of the Countess of Aberdeen on return from the Northwest, n.d.

11. French, *Ishbel*, pp. 151-15

12. Toronto Western Hospital, "Toronto Western Hospital 80th Birthday 1896-1976." Brochure; the information on the Euclid Avenue free dispensary is from a note listing the twelve pledging doctors, owned by Hudson Stowe.

13. Thompson, "Influence," p. 263

14. VUL ASG, box 1, microfilm, *Star*, 18 Feb. 1896.

15. Ibid., box 5, microfilm, plan of seating for the Mock Parliament.

16. Ibid., box 1, microfilm, *Star*, 18 Feb. 1896.

17. Thompson, "Influence," pp. 263-264.

18. VUL ASG, box 5, microfilm, letter to Lady Aberdeen, n.d.

19. French, *Ishbel*, pp. 223-224.

20. MacDonald, *Hoodless*, pp. 74-79, 168.

21. Information from Hudson Stowe.

22. National Council of Women of Canada. *Les Femmes du Canada leur Vie et leurs Oeuvres*. Book distributed at the Paris Exposition of 1900, publication committee on p. 70; Handbook of the National Council of Women. (Published by the Council, November 1899, central office, Ottawa), p. 4.

23. Ibid., pp. 60-61.

24. HJSG.

Chapter 11: The Torch is Passed

1. Ray, *Emily Stowe*, p. 41.

2. HJSG.

3. VUL ASG, box 1, microfilm, obituary, May 1903.

4. Ibid., box 5, microfilm.

5. Information from Hudson Stowe.

6. VUL ASG, box 5, microfilm.

7. Augusta Stowe Gullen, "Brief History," p. 5.

8. Hacker, *Indomitable*, p. 33.

9. Cleverdon, *Suffrage*, p. 28.

10. Ibid., p. 29.

11. VUL ASG, box 3, folder F.

12. Cleverdon, *Suffrage*, p. 30.

13. Thompson, "Influence," p. 265.

14. VUL ASG, box 5, microfilm, report by Jean Graham.

15. Thompson, "Influence," p. 265.

16. Middleton, *Toronto*, vol. 2, Chapter 12, "The Medical Profession of Toronto," by H.B. Anderson, M.D., pp. 622-623.

17. Thompson, "Influence," p. 265.

18. VUL ASG, box 5, microfilm, clipping.

19. Thompson, "Influence," pp. 265-266.

20. Cleverdon, *Suffrage*, p. 2.

21. OA, MU7320. Both pamphlets are in the Augusta Stowe Gullen envelope, as well as in the Victoria University Library.

22. VUL, ASG, box 3, folder B.

23. Ibid.

BIBLIOGRAPHY

Manuscripts

Few materials relating to Dr. Emily Stowe can be described as manuscripts. An important source is the papers and scrapbooks compiled by Dr. Stowe and her daughter, Dr. Stowe Gullen, now the property of Victoria University in Toronto and Wilfrid Laurier University in Waterloo. Most of the latter collection is also on microfilm at Victoria University, the page numbers often illegible. Much of the material is unidentified newspaper clippings, bearing few dates, although there are some personal letters.

True manuscripts are the letters of of Peter Lossing in the Baldwin Room, Metropolitan Toronto Library and in part of the Stowe collection in the Ontario Archives.

Fortunately, Dr. Stowe's life is not in the distant past; her grandson, Hudson Stowe, does not remember her, but he knew his aunt, Dr. Stowe Gullen, well. Hudson is also the family genealogist, as well as a source of many enlightening anecdotes.

The history of medicine has excited a lively interest over the generations. A wealth of material exists in the vast array of publications, recent and rare, in the Metropolitan Toronto Library and the Toronto Academy of Medicine Library.

Printed Publications

Abram, Ruth J. ed. *Send Us a Lady Physician: Women Doctors in America 1835-1920*. New York: W.W. Morton & Co., 1985.

Adams, J., M.D., M.C.P.S. Homeopathic Consulting Physician and Medical Electrician. *Electricity; its Mode of Action Upon the Human Frame and the Diseases in which it is Beneficial*. Toronto: 58 Bay St., n.d. Rare book, Toronto Academy of Medicine Library.

Bailey, Melville ed. *Dictionary of Hamilton Biography*. Hamilton: W.L. Griffin Ltd., 1981.

Brearley, David. *Hotbed of Treason: Norwich and the Rebellion of 1837*. Norwich: Norwich and District Historical Society, 1986.

Brotherton, John. "Evolution of Medical Practice." Nuffield Provincial Hospitals Trust. *Medical History and Medical Care: a Symposium of Perspectives*. London, New York, Toronto, 1971.

Canniff, William, M.D. *The Medical Profession in Upper Canada 1783-1850*. Toronto: William Briggs, 1894.

Clarke, Robert, and Others. *A Glimpse of the Past: Centennial History of Brantford and Brant County*. Brant County Historical Society, 1966.

Cleverdon, Catherine Lyle. *Woman Suffrage in Canada*. Toronto: University of Toronto Press, 1974.

Dorland, Arthur G. *Former Days and Quaker Ways*. Picton: Gazette Publishing Co. Ltd., 1965.

Ellis, David M., James A.Frost, Harold C. Syratt, Harry J. Carmen., *A History of New York State*. Ithica, N.Y.: Cornell University Press. New York State Historical Association, 1967.

Federation of Medical Women of Canada. *100 Years of Medicine 1849-1949*. Saskatoon: Modern Press Ltd., n.d.

Frost, Stanley Brice. *McGill University*. 2 vols. Montreal: McGill-Queen's Press, 1980.

Gibbon, John Murray, and Mary S. Mathewson, R.N., B.S. *Three Centuries of Canadian Nursing*. Toronto: MacMillan, 1947.

Godfrey, Charles M., M.D. *Medicine for Ontario: A History*. Belleville: Mika, 1979.

The Evolution of Medical Education in Ontario. Toronto: M.A. thesis for the Institute for the History and Philosophy of Science and Technology, University of Toronto, 1974. In the Toronto Academy of Medicine Library.

Guillet, Edwin C. *In the Cause of Education: Centennial History of the Ontario Educational Association 1861-1960*. Toronto: University of Toronto Press, 1960.

Gullet, D.W. *A History of Dentistry in Canada*. Toronto: University of Toronto Press, 1971.

Hacker, Carlotta. *The Indomitable Lady Doctors*. Toronto, Clarke Irwin, 1974.

Haggenson, C.D., and Lloyd E. B.Wyndham. *One Hundred Years of Medicine*. New York: Sheridan House, 1943.

Karr, William John, *The Training of Teachers in Ontario*. PhD thesis, Queen's University, 1916. Ottawa: R.J. Taylor, Printer, 1916.

Keers, R.Y. *Pulmonary Tuberculosis: A Journey down the Centuries*. London: Baillière Tindall,1978.

Kempster, Janet, and Muir, Gary. *Brantford: Grand River Crossing*. Windsor Publications (Canada) Ltd., 1986.

Koouwenhoven, John A. *The Columbia Historical Portrait of New York*. New York: Doubleday, 1953.

Lovejoy, Esther Phol., M.D. *Women Doctors of the World*. New York, Macmillan, 1957.

MacDermot, H.E., M.D. *One Hundred Years of Medicine in Canada 1867-1967*. Toronto: McClelland and Stewart, for the Canadian Medical Association, 1967.

MacDonald, Cheryl. *Adelaide Hoodless: Domestic Crusader*. Toronto: Dundurn, 1986.

MacDougall, Heather. "Public Health and the 'Sanitary Idea' in Toronto 1866-1890." InWendy Mitchenson and Janice Dicken McGinnis, eds. *Essays in the History of Canadian Medicine*, Toronto: McClelland and Stewart, 1988. "Toronto's Municipal Politics, the Canniff Years 1883-1890." *Bulletin of the History of Medicine*. #55, 1981.

Marks, Geoffrey, and Beatty, William K. *The Story of Medicine in America*. New York: Charles Scribner's Sons, 1973.

Middleton, Jesse Edgar. *The Municipality of Toronto: a History*. 3 vols. Toronto: The Dominion Publishing Co., 1923.

Morantz-Sanchez, Regina Markell. *Sympathy and Science: Women Physicians in American Medicine*. New York: Oxford, 1985.

Morgan, Henry J. *Canadian Men and Women of the Time*. 2 vols. Toronto: William Briggs, 1898.

Neatby, Hilda, Frederick W. Gibson and Roger Graham, eds. *Queen's University*. 2 vols. (vol. 1: 1841-1917; vol. 2: 1917-1961). Montreal: McGill-Queen's Press, 1978.

Poldon, Amelia. *The Amelia Poldon History of the Norwiches*. Norwich: Norwich and District Historical Society, 1985. Originally published as articles in the *Gazette*, Norwich, 1913-1914.

Prentice, Alison. *The School Promoters: Education and Social Class in Mid Nineteenth Century Upper Canada*. Toronto: McClelland and Stewart, 1977.

Ray, Janet. *Emily Stowe*. Don Mills: Fitzhenry and Whiteside, 1978. The Canadians Series.

Read, Colin, and Ronald J. Stagg. *The Rebellion of 1837*. Toronto: Champlain Society, 1985.

Read, Colin. *The Rising in Western Upper Canada 1837-8: The Duncombe Revolt and After*. Toronto: University of Toronto Press, 1982.

Riddell, Hon. William Renwick. "Popular Medicine in Upper Canada a Century Ago." Ontario Historical Society *Papers and Records*, vol. 25, 1929.

Seaborn, Edwin. *The March of Medicine in Western Ontario*. Toronto: Ryerson, 1944.

Shaw, Rosa L. *A History of the National Council of Women of Canada*. Toronto: Ryerson, 1957.

Sissons, Charles Bruce. *A History of Victoria University*. Toronto: University of Toronto Press, 1952.

Smith, William L. *Pioneers of Old Ontario*. London: Oxford University Press, 1923. Makers of Canada Series.

South Norwich Historical Society. *South of Sodom: The History of South Norwich*. Norwich, May 1983.

Spragge, George W. "The Trinity Medical College." *Ontario History*, vol. 58 #2 (June 1966).

Stafford, Ezra Hurlburt. *Medicine, Surgery and Hygiene in the Century*. London, Toronto, Philadelphia: Linscott Publishing Co., 1901.

Thompson, Joanne Emily. "The Influence of Dr. Emily Howard Stowe on the Woman Suffrage Movement in Canada." *Ontario History*, vol. 54 (Dec. 1962). M.A. Thesis, same title, Wilfred Laurier University, 1962.

Toronto Directories. Various years, Metropolitan Toronto Library.

Toronto (Ontario) Women's College Hospital. "The History of the Women's College Hospital." Toronto: n.d.

Tweedsmuir History of Mount Pleasant, Brant County. Microfilm of a scrapbook compiled by the Women's Institute, unpaginated, copy in Ontario Archives.

University of Toronto: the Librarian. *The University of Toronto. and its Colleges 1827-1906*. Toronto: University of Toronto Library, 1906.

Wallace, W. Stewart. *A History of the University of Toronto*. Toronto: University of Toronto Press, 1927.

Walsh, James Joseph. *History of Medicine in New York*. 5 vols. New York: National Americana Society Inc., 1919.

Wherrett, George Jasper. *The Miracle of the Empty Beds: A History of Tuberculosis in Canada*. Toronto: University of Toronto Press, 1977.

Young, James Harvey. *The Toadstool Millionaires: A Social History of Patent Medicine before Federal Regulation*. Princeton, N.J.: Princeton University Press, 1961.

INDEX